LOOKING WITH NEW EYES

My journey from
Bondage to Freedom

by
Annette Geroy

Belleville, Ontario, Canada

Looking With New Eyes

Copyright © 2006, Annette Geroy

All Scripture quotations, unless otherwise specified, are taken from the New International Version ®. NIV ® Copyright © 1995, 1996, 1998 by International Bible Society. Used by permission of Zondervan Publishing House. All rights reserved. • Scripture taken from *The Message*, copyright © by Eugene H. Peterson, 1993, 1994, 1995. Used by permission of NavPress Publishing Group. • Scripture quotations marked NASB are taken from the *New American Standard Bible*, copyright © The Lockman Foundation 1960, 1962, 1963, 1968, 1971, 1972, 1973. All rights reserved. • Scripture quotations marked KJV are taken from *The Holy Bible, King James Version*. Copyright © 1977, 1984, Thomas Nelson Inc., Publishers.

Library and Archives Canada Cataloguing in Publication

Geroy, Annette, 1948-

Looking with new eyes / Annette Geroy.

ISBN 1-55452-075-4 (pbk.)

ISBN 1-55452-106-8 (LSI/POD ed.)

1. Geroy, Annette, 1948-. 2. Adult child sexual abuse victims--United States--Biography. 3. Adult child sexual abuse victims--Religious life. I. Title.

BV4905.3.G47 2006   248.8'6   C2006-905164-X

For more information, please contact:

Annette Geroy
P.O. 293722
Kerrville, TX 78029

Guardian Books is an imprint of *Essence Publishing,* a Christian Book Publisher dedicated to furthering the work of Christ through the written word. For more information, contact:

20 Hanna Court, Belleville, Ontario, Canada K8P 5J2
Phone: 1-800-238-6376 • Fax: (613) 962-3055
E-mail: publishing@essencegroup.com
Web site: www.essencegroup.com/publishing

This book is dedicated to my mother
who was silent but has given me
permission to speak.

Special thanks to...

My husband, Dan, who walked alongside me through the healing process and supported, wholeheartedly, the writing of this book.

My children: Jude and Jane, Ginny and Robert... for your love, understanding and encouragement.

Betty Hendrick, Beth McKenzie, Ann Strieber and Penny Williams for sharing your time and expertise to help shape this book.

Those who have prayed, read and encouraged me continuously throughout the writing process:

Hershel and Shannon Reid, Blake and Beth McKenzie, Peggy Maxfeldt, Juli Hobin, Joann Stone, Leigh Hebert, Mary Lou Ticknor, Kathleen Maxwell, Vickie Byrd, David and Cindy Danielson.

Pattie Kline, my college roommate, who has walked with me through all these years...thanks.

And to Phil Bob Borman, whose beautiful drawings complete the picture the Lord gave me for this book. Thanks for listening to his voice.

Table of Contents

Introduction

Looking With New Eyes is the story of how Jesus replaced the lies planted deeply in my heart—with truth. It is the story of my release from the bondage of sexual abuse. If you were sexually abused as a child, this book was written to bring you hope. There is freedom in Christ, but sometimes we need help discovering how to find that freedom. You may be a pastor, a counselor, a friend, or a spouse of someone who was sexually abused who is looking for fresh direction. In the pages of this book you will discover principles of prayer that can open doors to God's great power to redeem and restore the wounded heart. He did it for me. He can do it for you!

I discovered this poem in the devotional book, *Streams In the Desert.* It expresses, so poignantly, my purpose in writing this book as I "call back" my encouragement to each of you.

If you have gone a little way ahead of me, call back—
It will cheer my heart and help my feet along the stony track;

And if, perhaps, Faith's light is dim, because the oil is low,
Your call will guide my lagging course as wearily I go.
Call back, and tell me that He went with you into the storm;
Call back, and say He kept you when the forest's roots were torn;
That, when the heavens' thunder and earthquake shook the hill,
He bore you up and held you where the lofty air was still.
Oh friend, call back, and tell me for I cannot see your face;
They say it glows with triumph, and your feet sprint in the race;
But there are mists between us and my spirit eyes are dim,
And I cannot see the glory, though I long for word of Him.
But if you'll say He heard you when your prayer was but a cry,
And if you'll say He saw you through the night's sin-darkened sky—
If you have gone a little way ahead, oh friend, call back—
It will cheer my heart and help my feet along the stony track.[1]

What would I call back? I believe the Lord has been giving us "new eyes" to see and ears to hear a more complete message of healing over the last several years, even though the way to healing has always been available to us through the Scriptures. He is shining light on the pathway to healing and inviting us to follow him, saying, *This is the way; walk in it* (Isaiah 30:21). Sexual abuse is now being seen for what it is— a devastating epidemic. But this epidemic has a balm and a cure through the healing power of Jesus Christ!

There are a number of reasons why *Looking With New Eyes* can become a stepping stone to healing for many:

○ There is currently a great stirring of the Holy Spirit to heal and to purify the Bride of Christ, the Church. This Spirit-led movement is calling us to greater honesty, openness and freedom with each other and the world.

○ Through new technology we have instant access to a wide range of information. Tales of sexual abuse, which were once taboo, are often the topic of television talk shows. This brings the issue of abuse to light, but may also cause us to become desensitized to the monstrously degrading impact sexual abuse has on a child. Simply *exposing* the abuser is not enough to bring healing. Unless the story of sexual abuse is coupled with the healing power of Jesus Christ, we are left with only hopeless victims.

○ The myth that sexual abuse is not an issue that impacts the lives of Christians has been forever shattered!

○ Most importantly, for me, the Lord has brought me through a process of deep inner healing. He has set me on a path of ministering to other women who have been sexually abused–women who are still living in bondage.

Over the years I spent time with a number of different counselors, slowly exposing the truth of my abuse. These were good people who desired to see me free of the pain. In 2002, at the age of fifty-four, I finally found what I had been looking for all those years. Over a period of three years, the Lord began bringing light to the deep-rooted lies I believed about myself and him, showing me his truth and setting me on the road to freedom. *Looking With New Eyes* is the story of my healing journey.

Embedded in boxed text in the following chapters are scriptural principles for healing that will hold true for *your* healing journey, even though our stories may be very different. I have also included what I feel are necessary components of the process of healing. Accompanying my story are images of an old house hemmed in, or veiled, by an overgrowth of trees. The trees represent the lies the Lord had to uproot in my heart and mind so that I could begin to see myself from his perspective. The process of "uprooting the lies" was painful, but necessary. Scripture says *A veil covers their hearts. But whenever anyone turns to the Lord, the veil is taken away* (2 Corinthians 3:15-16).

I also formed life habits for survival when "hemmed in" by lies about my value and worth as a result of being victimized. Dallas Willard says, "Rejection is so gut-wrenching because our spiritual selves are designed to live with grace"[2]—God's grace. There is no grace in sexual abuse. The evil one desired to keep me enslaved to the lies, but through Jesus Christ came healing and freedom. Getting to the place of freedom required a commitment on my part, sensitivity to the leading of the Holy Spirit, and a willingness to visit some really difficult memories.

Living and walking in freedom require a plan—a plan to continue to choose to believe the truths the Lord has shown me. Today I walk in freedom!

For several years I have worked as a prayer minister with other women who have suffered sexual abuse. The Lord is always gracious in uprooting the lies they believe and replacing them with the light of his truth. Their freedom, like mine, is life-changing, and they are becoming instruments of his grace to those around them. Jesus wants to bring healing and freedom to you, as well.

Are you brave enough to begin the journey to healing and freedom? Then look and listen as I "call back" to you.

Chapter One

*The Lord was offering me a chance to
be free. I had to be willing.*

The Invitation

*The Lord your God will circumcise your hearts
and the hearts of your descendants so that you
may love him with all your soul and live.*

DEUTERONOMY 30:6

For many years my soul was bound with cords of fear and shame. The fear taught me to be self-controlled and controlling of others. The shame separated me from God—kept me from being able to love him with *all my soul*. In the quiet recesses of my heart I did not believe him to be trustworthy. In my mind I knew that I was his, but I was not living in his freedom. There was no abundant life. *I have come that they may have life, and have it to the full* (John 10:10). Having become a Christian at the age of eight and having spent many years "in church," I knew the message of hope and peace and abundant living, but I had only seen glimpses of these things in my own life. I had looked for them in my husband, children, profession, friends, in church and Bible study, even in counseling. But I was never free because the cords were binding my heart. I did not recognize fear and shame as the emotions that held me captive.

The Lord confronted me with a challenge similar to the one in Deuteronomy 30:19:

> *I have set before you life and death, blessings and curses. Now choose life, so that you and your children may live and that you may love the LORD your God, listen to his voice, and hold fast to him.*

The Lord was offering me a chance to be free. I had to be willing. He alone was the one who could circumcise my heart, to remove the foreskin that had become my shield against the pain—physical, emotional and spiritual. Through the writing of Frances Roberts came these words:

> *The limitations of your natural vision will be no handicap. The Spirit is not detained by the flesh. The Spirit will move in spite of the flesh and will accomplish a renewal and do a work of re-creating, so that the newly liberated creature will rise up in virgin life, starting out upon a ministry the foundation of which no man has laid. It will be a path of holiness, a way of miracles, and a life of glory. You will see My shining smile.*
>
> *Nothing will be required of you but obedience. You will follow the call of the Spirit and not search for the path; for the way will be laid down before you as you tread. Wherever you stop, there will the path stop also. Whenever you walk in faith, the way will be made clear before you.*

Be as a young child and step out in confidence, knowing that with your hand in Mine you will be always safe, and blessings will attend you. [1]

With a wounded, trembling heart I accepted the Lord's challenge.

I am sharing my story so that you may be encouraged to allow him to circumcise *your* heart as well. I can guarantee the journey will be painful. Even so, if you are willing to *listen to him* and *hold fast to him*, the cords that hold you in bondage will be cut, the shield will be removed, and you will learn that Jesus is trustworthy and loving, tender and kind. Your walk with him will become an intimate relationship, and the Lord's love will fill the gaping holes in your wounded heart. I "call back" to you.

The righteous cry out, and the LORD hears them; he delivers them from all their troubles. The LORD is close to the brokenhearted and saves those who are crushed in spirit (Psalm 34:17-18).

I now live in his freedom! He has re-created my broken heart. He has brought peace to my soul. He has called me his "precious jewel." He has given me words to speak. With Jeremiah I must say, *His word is in my heart like a fire, a fire shut up in my bones. I am weary of holding it in; indeed, I cannot* (Jeremiah 20:9).

The Spirit of the Sovereign LORD is on me, because the LORD has anointed me to preach good news to the poor. He has sent me to bind up the brokenhearted, to pro-

claim freedom for the captives, and release from darkness for the prisoners, to proclaim the year of the LORD's favor and the day of vengeance of our God, to comfort all who mourn, and provide for those who grieve in Zion—to bestow on them a crown of beauty instead of ashes, the oil of gladness instead of mourning, and a garment of praise instead of a spirit of despair. They will be called oaks of righteousness, a planting of the LORD for the display of his splendor (Isaiah 61:1-3).

My writing will often be graphic and harshly honest because you need to know that I know your pain. I have been there. Memories will be stirred up. If you and the Lord have dealt with those memories, there will be rejoicing. If you have not, there will be pain. However, in the pages of this book you will discover an avenue to freedom.

Go get a box of tissues, find a place to be alone with God, and prepare to shed tears of pain and joy as we walk through this together.

Chapter One

Reflecting on God's Light

1. The emotions of fear and shame held my heart in bondage. Do any of the following emotions seem to have a hold on your life?

   A sense of being abandoned
   Feeling powerless
   Not having been validated or affirmed
   Fear
   Confusion
   Hopelessness
   A sense of being tainted
   Helplessness

2. If you were to draw a picture of the condition of your heart, how would it look?

3. Re-read the Jeremiah 61:1-3 passage in this chapter. As you read, what thoughts come to mind?

_____

_____

_____

_____

_____

_____

_____

_____

_____

_____

Chapter Two

Uncovered was exactly how I felt—
uncovered, unprotected
and unworthy.

Prisoner's Clothes

One day I was driving to work when my eyes were drawn to the figure of a man pushing a lawn mower across the grassy area in front of the Department of Public Safety. He was dressed in the bold black-and-white-striped uniform of a prisoner, topped with an iridescent orange vest. He stopped behind the mower for a moment, straightening his vest in the same manner a gentleman might straighten his dinner jacket. The scene struck me as being incongruous, almost laughable. And yet, it was a picture of how we live our lives. Those around us recognize that we are a prisoner to something in our past, while we tuck and preen hoping no one else sees our vulnerability and pain.

For many years I was a prisoner to emotions that were tied to lies I believed about myself. The *lies* I accepted as *truth* were the result of having been sexually abused. I believed the abuse was my own fault; that there was nothing in me that was worthy of love. The black cords encircling my heart were excruciatingly painful as I unconsciously grieved the loss of my childhood, my innocence.

In his book, *Woman, Thou Art Loosed*, T.D. Jakes defines abuse as "abnormal use." He goes on to say, "I think it is interesting that when the Bible talks about sexual abuse within a family it uses the word 'uncover.' Sexual abuse violates the covering of a family and the responsible persons whom we look to for guidance. This stripping away of right relationship leaves us exposed to the infinite reality of corrupt, lustful imaginations. Like fruit peeled too soon, it is damaging to uncover what God had wanted to remain protected!"[1]

None of you shall approach to any that is near of kin to him, to uncover their nakedness. I am the LORD (Leviticus 18:6 KJV).

> **Principle**
>
> *My present situation was not the primary source of my emotional pain.*[2]

Uncovered was exactly how I felt—uncovered, unprotected and unworthy. Because of those feelings, I had learned to be ever-diligent in protecting myself and my family. These behavioral patterns had become the norm. Anger would quickly surface when I felt rejected. The typical pattern included ranting to some dear person who would listen or withdrawing into desperate despair. On the outside I kept my iridescent orange vest (my covering) perfectly in place while on the inside there was hidden, controlled anguish.

Eventually, I began working with a Christian counselor in a desire to diffuse some of the hurt and pain. He used traditional therapy coupled with Scripture. As we examined some Scriptural truths about forgiveness, I began to feel that I needed to forgive my earthly father before I could move on with my life. It was the right thing to do. However, there was a problem. My father had been in a nursing home for almost ten years, his body and mind becoming less and less functional with the terrible progression of Parkinson's disease. He had not recognized me for at least three years. There was no possibility of open communication between the two of us.

After counsel, prayer and much soul searching, I finally decided the only way I could bring closure with my father was to write him a letter. I swirled around in a sea of anxiety over the day to come when I would write to my father about the abuse he inflicted on me. It took almost six months to compose my thoughts. I did not want to have memories of having written that letter at my desk or dining table, so I chose a place away from my home. I wrote down all the things my father had done that I knew to be inappropriate and hurtful—the sexual molestation, the sordid stories, the unrelenting control, the verbal abuse. I expressed my desire to forgive him because I knew that he, too, had suffered injury. I told him that I could forgive because I had experienced the love of my Heavenly Father and had a healthy relationship with him. I expressed my sadness at only being able to remember the awful things he had done—that the good times faded from view in light of his abuse.

The letter, representing my closure with my dad, was sealed in a separate envelope and mailed to my mother. My father's health was declining rapidly, so I asked her not to read it but to place it in my father's casket upon his death.

Although I had done the right thing, in my heart I still felt like a prisoner.

Reflecting on God's Light

1. Are you walking around in prisoner's clothes? On the stripes write the words that describe the emotions which hold you in bondage.

2. On the "orange vest" below, write words to describe what you do when you need to feel in control.

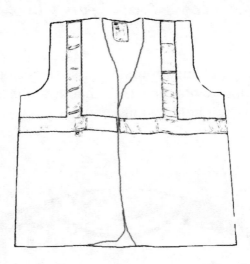

3. What might be some options for confronting your abuser?

_____

_____

_____

_____

4. What kind of responses might you expect if you confront your abuser?

_____

_____

_____

Chapter Three

*It was just something that
had happened.*

Pigeonholed Emotions

*Turn to me and be gracious to me, for I am
lonely and afflicted. The troubles of my heart
have multiplied; free me from my anguish.
Look upon my affliction and my distress
and take away all my sins.*

PSALM 25:16-18

I t seems odd to me that we think (or have
been taught) that the level of pain in our lives
is directly proportional to the number and
type of sins we commit. I am not saying that
sin does not create consequences. It does. However,
I always thought that my shame, loneliness and pain
had to do with things I was doing wrong—my sin. I
never even considered the possibility of those feelings being the consequence of something that was
done *to* me.

I would describe myself as a person who
"pigeonholes" emotions. Let me explain. Pigeons
roost in a structure called a dovecote. There is an
opening called a pigeonhole, usually in the top,
which allows the birds to move in and out of the
dovecote. When a bird squeezes its body through the
"pigeonhole" for the night, it can no longer be seen.

For me, when shame or loneliness turned into *anguish*, I simply *pigeonholed* it! In psychological terms this would be called suppressing your emotions. I would suppress my emotions and ask God to *take away my sin*. It was only after years of wrestling that I discovered I was asking for the wrong thing.

> **Principle**
>
> *My present situation triggers familiar painful emotions from earlier events. The situations only need to be "similar" in order to tap into the historical pain.* [1]

On a conscious level I knew that I had been molested by my father, but there were no emotions! It was just something that had happened. A counselor finally helped me put the label *sexual abuse* to my father's actions. He also asked where my mother was during that time. He implied that she, as the other adult in the house, was responsible for not intervening if she was aware of what was happening to me. I have to tell you, that thought was completely foreign to me! It had never occurred to me that she, too, was responsible. My feelings of loneliness turned into a deep sense of abandonment. Those pigeonholed emotions began to stir.

About this same time, my husband had been going through some extensive counseling training with the Christian ministry where we served. He tried sharing some of the techniques with me and got an unexpected reaction! The idea was to allow you to *revisit* the emotions surrounding those times when you were physically or emotionally wounded. As you experience the emotions of that painful situation, you ask God to show you the lies Satan planted in your mind and heart about your value and worth. We were both real novices with this prayer ministry process, so when Dan asked me to identify the implanted lies, I just kept saying, "All I see is the *truth*!" The *truth* that I had been abused, the *truth* that I had been abandoned, and the *truth* that I had been left to handle things on my own was all that I could see. I began to cry as I revisited the scene.

In my mind's eye I could see my mother and father's bedroom—the gray-green walls, the windows, the bed. I could hear the latch on the door snap into place after being summoned into the room by my father. I could feel my father's hands touching my body in places he should not have been touching. I could remember anxiety building as I pleaded with him to stop, twisting and turning but being unable to break his grip. I remembered screaming to my mother, "Mama, make him stop! Make him stop!" There was only silence. I knew she was in the house. I knew that she heard, and yet she did nothing. She abandoned me. I was hurt, panicked and angry! I was powerless. My only option was to fight, to assure my safety by assuming control. At age fourteen I became the *adult*, making a vow never to be left vulnerable again.

Now, for the first time in my life, I was angry with my father for molesting me and my mother for abandoning me. I cried. I cursed. I ranted. Suppressed emotions boiled out. It felt as though the *troubles of my heart had multiplied*, but the *truth* of the situation had simply come clear. As I allowed the pain of the loss to finally surface and flow out, my husband held me and soothed me and cried with me. Until then, my wounds had continued to fester and poison my life even though I thought I had things *under control*.

It has been said, "A wound unwept is a wound unhealed."[2]

That day, I wept!

Chapter Three

Reflecting on God's Light

> *Principle:* My present situation triggers familiar painful emotions from earlier events. The situations only need to be "similar" in order to tap into the historical pain.

1. Are there emotions that you seem to experience over and over again? Do you seem to have the same argument with your spouse/child/parent without coming to any resolution? What are you feeling when this happens?

_____

_____

_____

_____

2. Can you identify the source of your pain? What is it?

_____

_____

_____

_____

3. Have you taken time to grieve the loss of your innocence? Why might that be an important thing for you to do? (Ask the Lord to show you where to begin.)

_____

_____

_____

_____

Chapter Four

I found myself angry with God.

Where Were You, Lord?

> *So justice is far from us, and righteousness does not reach us. We look for light, but all is darkness; for brightness, but we walk in deep shadows. Like the blind we grope along the wall, feeling our way like men without eyes.*
>
> ISAIAH 59:9-10

In June of the same year the truth of my abuse became real to me, our ministry staff was involved in counseling training. We were watching a series of tapes. The speaker had worked with victims of sexual abuse for a number of years. He had prayed for and been given a different, more effective approach through which these abuse victims were coming to a place of real healing—real recovery. Unlike cognitive therapy, which deals primarily with changing thinking patterns, this prayer ministry centers on the heart and the healing of wounds.

At one point the speaker was describing some typical reactions

Principle

Everything has a source and origin. The present is a reflection of the past.[1]

of a sexual abuse victim. He described a woman jerking away when her husband walked up behind her to put his arms around her. My jaw dropped! I had done that so many times! I never really understood why, and my husband always took it as an affront—as rejection. For the first time I began to understand that my actions in my adult life were bound, in part, to the abuse that took place during my childhood. I was a well-informed adult, so this should not have been new information. Yet, somehow, I was just beginning to make the connection. In my *head* I had known there were repercussions of abuse, but I had never fully identified them in myself. In my heart I was still that hurting little girl, but I had her tucked away—hidden.

I began to seriously reach out for healing. In my mind, I went back to that gray-green bedroom. I experienced the shock, embarrassment and anger, again. I looked honestly at the wounds in my heart and the questions in my head.

I could hear Satan saying:

"Why did you walk into that room, again?"

"You weren't a child, anymore. What were you thinking?"

"What did you do to arouse him?"

"You are the only one this ever happened to."

"You must not be worth much if your own father would treat you this way."

"The only way you are going to survive is by helping yourself (assuming control)."

"Ha! Ha! Ha! You felt the arousal."

"You are dirty."

"You are a stupid girl."

"You aren't worth loving."

I could also hear my screams for help. I remembered that the last time it happened my mother *did* come—she banged on the locked door, yelling, "What's going on in there?"

My father lied to her.

I found myself angry with God. *"Where were you, Lord?"* became a consuming question. I didn't understand why he had not protected me and realized that I did not trust him because of that. Again I begged, *"Where were you, Lord?"* During a time of prayer ministry, he showed me. In my mind's eye I could see the Lord standing by the window, his arm outstretched as though to intervene. He was crying; crying for me, crying for my father, crying for my mother standing outside the door. What was happening was not *his* desire for any of us.

> *The Lord looked and was displeased that there was no justice...he was appalled that there was no one to intervene* (Isaiah 59:15-16).

My father made a choice to molest me. My mother made a choice to believe my father's lies. I made a choice to be in control (something that, over time, developed into my personal sense of security—my idol). None of it was *God's* choice for our best. He had given us, as his creation, the ability to choose sin. He anguished over what was happening, but he did not intervene.

According to Scripture, we are caught in the middle of a cosmic conflict between good and evil. We live in a *fallen* world. Just as Adam and Eve were lured away by the serpent, Satan, from obeying the voice of God concerning the tree of knowledge (Genesis 3:23), we are also lured into believing his lies. We bear the mark of their sinful choice and we struggle. We know that bad things happen to the very people who were designed to be the heart of God. From the human perspective, it makes no sense. Our hope, however, lies in the fact that the plans of the Lord are never destroyed, regardless of the things that happen to us. The Word says *The plans of the Lord stand firm forever* (Psalm 33:11).

Isaiah 52:10 reads, *The LORD will lay bare his holy arm in the sight of all the nations and the ends of the earth will see the salvation of our God.*

Isaiah 59:16 says, *So his own arm worked salvation for him, and his own righteousness sustained him.*

The Lord's perfect plan was for my earthly father to provide a spiritual covering for our entire family—protecting, providing for our physical and spiritual needs and sending us out into life holy and whole. His plan for my mother was to assist my father and to protect and nurture her children. However, like many women in abusive situations, she felt trapped in a tangled web and saw no way out. Neither my father nor my mother was following the Lord's plan. Things were not *working together for good*. So with an outstretched arm he took hold and began to establish his perfect plan in a different way. *The Lord has sworn by his right hand and by his mighty arm; Never again...never again* (Isaiah 62:8).

For me, the physical sexual abuse stopped that day, in that gray-green room, when I was fourteen.

Reflecting on God's Light

> **Principle:** Everything has a source and origin.
> The present is a reflection of the past.

1. Read the opening words from Isaiah 59:9-10. Ask Jesus to show you one thing (wound or emotion) that keeps you *walking in deep shadows...like men without eyes.*

   _____

   _____

2. If you are having thoughts that are discouraging or belittling, those words are *not* coming from Jesus. What is Satan whispering in your ear?

   _____

   _____

   _____

   _____

3. Do you think God's plan for your life can be defeated by your choice or the choice of others? Use a concordance to look up the words "choice" and "plan."

_____

_____

_____

_____

_____

4. If you are an abuse survivor, what was the extent of the sexual abuse you experienced? Perpetrator? Length of time? Memories?

_____

_____

_____

_____

_____

_____

_____

_____

_____

Chapter Five

Satan's greatest tool—
the whispered lie.

Satan's Tactics

*The great dragon was hurled down—that
ancient serpent called the devil, or Satan,
who leads the whole world astray.*

REVELATION 12:9

S atan has only a limited number of tactics to use as he *prowls around like a roaring lion looking for someone to devour* (1 Peter 5:8). He is desperate to destroy us. Our very image reminds him that he is *not* God, that he is defeated. He lashes out in vindictive anguish to keep us from knowing, fully, the love of our heavenly Father. How does he do this? The tactics he used with Adam and Eve worked so well that he continues to use the same ones, over and over again. He was *subtle*—he used a serpent to approach Adam and Eve. He was a *coward*—he assaulted the woman rather than the man. His evil nature was exposed in that he *lied* to her. He incited Eve to commit not a *moral* sin, but a *spiritual* sin—breaking God's command. His real object of attack was God's Word![1]

1. Satan lies to us.

One of the most powerful scenes from *The Passion of the Christ* is the opening, where Jesus was in the Garden of Gethsemane praying. As Jesus poured out his heart, sweating drops of blood at the thought of a momentary separation from the Father, Satan stood on the sidelines watching. When Jesus collapsed, Satan began to whisper "Do you really believe that one can bear the full burden of sin?" "No man can carry this burden, I tell you." "It is far too heavy." "Saving their souls is too costly." He hissed, "No one. Ever. No. Never." He questioned, "Who is your father?" "Who are *you*?"[2] Lies. Lies. Lies. Persistent lies.

I believe this scene graphically depicts Satan's greatest tool, the whispered lie. How did Jesus respond? For a time, he ignored Satan as he submitted his will to the Father's. Satan waited quietly, the nuances of his expressions saying, "Perhaps I have caught him off guard. Perhaps he will listen to me." But when Jesus turned and looked at him with contempt, Satan knew he was defeated! Crushed!

If Satan lied to Jesus, who are we to think he would not lie to us?

2. Satan starts when we are very young.

In a recent video, *Broken Trust,* prepared by the American Association of Christian Counselors, Dan Allender gave these statistics: 52 percent of all women and 33 percent of all men have experienced some form of sexual abuse before the age of eighteen.

Allender divides abuse into two large categories:
• when an older more powerful person uses a less powerful person for their own sexual pleasure,
• when a slightly older child introduces a younger child to sexual issues.

He further categorizes abuse into *"physical contact"* and *"interactions."* Physical contact may include anything from simple touching to forced intercourse or rape. Interaction does not have to involve touching but may involve being visually observed in a sensual manner, verbally abused through seductive conversation, or experiencing emotional incest when a child is drawn into a surrogate adult role (a daughter takes on the role of "mother" or a son the role of "father").

Regardless of the circumstances, Dr. Allender says, *"Abuse is abuse is abuse. All abuse is damaging."*[3]

Dr. Ed Smith examines the connection between our emotions and our experiences. He says,

When information comes to us through experience, our minds couple it with emotion. This emotionally charged information (whether positive or negative) becomes the primary source upon which we rely for future experiential decisions and responses. Once the original experience is recorded, with its emotional response and belief interpretation, it changes very little over time, even with the accumulation of additional data that is contrary.[4]

Let's say, for example, a child gets separated from his mother at the grocery store. In his innocent mind, the child might interpret this experience by thinking, "I am all alone. I have been abandoned.

There must be something wrong with me." This thought will produce emotions such as insecurity and fear of rejection or abandonment. When a new experience arises in which he finds himself alone, he will return to (remember) the same thoughts and experience the same emotional response: "Something is wrong with me; I am all alone." Later in life he may learn the scripture, *I am with you always* (Matthew 28:20) and believe it in his head. But in his heart he is still that little child, fearful, abandoned and alone.

As children, we are more vulnerable to the emotions associated with experiences because we are not mentally mature enough to separate truth from a misconception or lie.

In *Woman Thou Art Loosed,* T. D. Jakes describes children as "living epistles that should stand as evidence to the future that the past made some level of contribution." He refers to David's declaration in the Psalms:

> *Sons are a heritage from the LORD,*
> *children a reward from him.*
> *Like arrows in the hands of a warrior*
> *are sons born in one's youth.*
> *Blessed is the man*
> *whose quiver is full of them.*
> *They will not be put to shame*
> *when they contend with their enemies in the gate*
> (Psalm 127:3-5).

Jakes continues, "It is for the arrows of this generation that we must pray. Not all of them, but some of them, have been broken in the quiver!" He goes on to say:

> *I write to every empty-eyed child I have ever seen sit at my desk with tears and trembling lips struggling to tell their unmentionable secret.*
>
> *I write to the trembling voice of every caller who spoke into a telephone the secret they could not keep and could not tell.*
>
> *I write to every husband who holds a woman every night who was a child lost in space, a rosebud crushed before you met her, a broken arrow shaking in the quiver.*
>
> *And I write to every lady who hides behind her silk dresses and leather purses a terrible secret that makeup can't seem to cover and long showers will not wash.*
>
> *Today the Church must realize that the adult problems we are fighting to correct are often rooted in the ashes of childhood experiences. Our patients' wounds are in the heart. We don't need medicine; we need miracles. We need to share God-given, biblical answers to troubling questions as we deal with the highly sensitive areas of sexually abused children.*[5]

My immediate response was that T.D. Jakes was furious about the issues of childhood sexual abuse, and I loved him for it! Finally, someone cared enough to shout about it!

3. Satan uses the fact that we are "emotional beings" to lure us into questioning God's character.

If Satan can convince us that God will not protect us, that God is not good, that the wicked will prevail and that God does not really care, then he has accomplished much in his attempt to destroy the image of God in us. Because we are emotional beings, Satan has access to our minds and hearts. Emotions are the doors through which he can gain access. The choice may be someone else's or our own, but we are most vulnerable when we are young. It is the responsibility of parents to guard and protect the hearts of their children. Sometimes even their most diligent efforts fail. Sometimes they are the cause of the pain or injury, which causes us to question God.

> *"Although feelings often seem unpredictable and irrational, they are neither random nor unprovoked. Different people react differently to different situations, but due to our common heritage as persons made in the image of God, we share some predictable patterns."*[6]

❍ What is our emotional reaction when someone attacks us? We either return the attack in anger or retreat in fear.

❍ How do we respond to abandonment? We either cling desperately in a jealous rage or withdraw in despair.

❍ What do we do when someone loves us but we view that love as unbelievable because we do not feel worthy? We wall ourselves in with skepticism and contempt or flee from the need it exposes within us by withdrawing completely.

Our response to others opens the door to our

?

win?

...nstance of our lives, God is
...relationship with him. From
...tion was fresh and he sought
...sired (and still seeks) to have us

4. Satan uses the weak and wounded to violate the
most intimate part of our physical being, our
sexuality.

*The body is not meant for sexual immorality, but for the
Lord, and the Lord for the body...Flee from sexual
immorality. All other sins a man commits are outside
his body, but he who sins sexually sins against his own
body. Do you not know that your body is a temple of the
Holy Spirit, who is in you, whom you have received
from God?* (1 Corinthians 6:13,18,19).

Through childhood sexual abuse, Satan's great
sacrilege against the temple of God, children are
taught that nothing is holy or sacred. This, too, is a lie!

*Do not defile yourselves in any of these ways, because
this is how the nations that I am going to drive out*

before you became defiled. Even the land was defiled; so I punished it for its sin, and the land vomited out its inhabitants. But you must keep my decrees and my laws...If you defile the land, it will vomit you out as it vomited out the nations that were before you (Leviticus 18:24,25,28).

5. Satan catches us off guard when we are vulnerable: having suffered a loss, are alone and rejected, being consumed by illness or feeling powerless to make a change in our lives.

In Psalm 38, King David voices the desperation we sometimes feel when we are vulnerable:

For I am about to fall,
and my pain is ever with me.
I confess my iniquity;
I am troubled by my sin.
Many are those who are my vigorous enemies;
those who hate me without reason are numerous.
Those who repay my good with evil
slander me when I pursue what is good.
O LORD, do not forsake me;
be not far from me, O my God.
Come quickly to help me,
O Lord my Savior (Psalm 38:17-22).

Satan lies to us. He is intent on destroying us. He *is* the enemy of our lives—spiritually, emotionally and physically. Yet, with the desperate and vulnerable psalmist we can declare with confidence:

We wait in hope for the LORD;
he is our help and our shield.
In him our hearts rejoice,
for we trust in his holy name.
May your unfailing love rest upon us, O LORD,
even as we put our hope in you (Psalm 33:20-22).

Chapter Five

Reflecting on God's Light

1. Were you surprised by Allender's statistics about the number of men and women who are sexually abused? Why?

_____

_____

_____

_____

2. As you read through his description of the things that are considered abuse, could you identify any that you have experienced? What were they?

_____

_____

_____

_____

3. How does Satan attempt to lure us away from God?

_____

_____

_____

_____

Chapter Six

*I could not identify exactly
how I was feeling.*

My Most Vulnerable Moment

*My sheep listen to my voice; I know them,
and they follow me. I give them eternal life,
and they shall never perish; no one can
snatch them out of my hand.*

JOHN 10:27-28

We need to trust the Lord. We were designed to trust him! God must be experienced before he can be understood and trusted, but suppressed memories and emotions undermine our willingness to open our hearts to him. Luke 4:18 speaks of Jesus bringing *good news to the poor...freedom for the prisoners...sight for the blind...and release to the oppressed.* Jesus didn't just preach to the intellect, he touched the hearts and lives of hurting people. Those who were willing to risk a relationship with Jesus *experienced* his love!

I had been unconsciously bound for so long by Satan's lies that the image of Jesus in that bedroom, crying over us (me, my father and my mother), made me want to run to him. Like a petulant child, I wanted all the cords of worthlessness and shame cut immediately. I wanted freedom and I was willing to ask him to fulfill his promises! *O people of Zion...you will weep no more. How gracious he will be when you cry for help! As soon as he hears, he will answer you* (Isaiah 30:19). I wanted it *now*! But the Lord knew I was not ready to bear the whole truth all at once. So for me, at least, he has been cutting the cords one at a time.

Another conscious memory had popped out of the pigeonhole. With the help of a counselor/prayer minister, I began to explore the implications of what I came to see as my *most vulnerable moment*. In this memory I was ten years old. I had recently started my first menstrual cycle, and my body was beginning to mature and take on new shapes. After taking a bath, I was examining those curious developments when I suddenly became aware of my father standing outside the door. The door was locked, but there was a space between the door and the facing that provided a limited view into the bathroom. With five of us in a house with one bathroom, we all used that space at one time or another to see if the bathroom was occupied. But this was no innocent "peek." He was there several minutes, standing close and watching me.

I was naked, alone and exposed! He was gawking, and I felt guilty. Was there something about my self examination that aroused him? I was horrified at the thought! I felt dirty, used, violated! I was isolated, trapped with an audience, raped by his looking at me that way. He left quietly without saying a word, taking my innocence with him.

I left that counseling session emotionally raw. I could not identify exactly how I was feeling. The questions remained: "How could a father look on his daughter with such wanton disregard?" "Was there something in me that encouraged his behavior?" As I wrestled for a word that would describe my deepest feeling, I could hear Satan's silent scream, "Ann, you are *unlovable!*" "There is nothing lovely, nothing worthy of love, nothing!" I felt damaged, bruised beyond repair.

Henri Nouwen once wrote,

> *Constantly I am tempted to wallow in my own lostness and lose touch with my original goodness, my God-given humanity, my basic blessedness, and thus allow the powers of death to take charge. This happens over and over again whenever I say to myself: "I am no good. I am useless. I am worthless. I am unlovable. I am a nobody."...Many people live with this dark inner sense of themselves. They let the darkness absorb them so completely that there is no light left...They might not kill themselves physically, but spiritually they are no longer alive. They have given up faith in their original goodness and, thus, also in their Father who has given them their humanity. But when God created man and woman in his own image, he saw that "it was good" and, despite the dark voices, no man or woman can ever change that.*[1]

Like Nouwen, I had believed the lie.

I had worked all my life to be "lovable." I responded with contempt when someone's actions or words implied that I was not worthy of being acknowledged or recognized (not necessarily praised—just *seen as being worth seeing*). I had never associated this outward, ungracious, sinful behavior with the thought of being closed up in that awful bathroom—alone, afraid, unlovable. But there it was, and it too was ugly!

In anguish I began to sob. I cried uncontrollably: tears for my loss of innocence, tears for my father's personal pain, tears for those I had devastated over the years with my anger and sharp-tongued responses. With a sadness of heart that I did not think could be healed, I laid myself before the Lord.

> ## Principle
>
> *If I try to resolve my present conflict without finding healing for my past wounds, I will find, at best, only temporary relief. However, if I allow Jesus to heal my past, my present is redeemed![2]*

I begged for the Lord's covering of that ten-year-old girl. I asked to be released from my obsession with protecting myself through aggressive behavior.

I prayed: *Turn your steps toward these everlasting ruins, all this destruction the enemy has brought on the sanctuary* (Psalm 74:3).

I read: *Unless you turn and become like little children you will never enter the kingdom of heaven* (Matthew 18:3).

I prayed: *I cried out to God for help; I cried out to God to hear me. When I was in distress, I sought the Lord; at night I stretched out untiring hands and my soul refused to be comforted* (Psalm 77:1-2).

I read: "...the joys of the *second childhood:* comfort, mercy, an ever clearer vision of God...a place where I can live without obsessions and compulsions."[3] (emphasis added)

I prayed: "Lord, help me move out of that bathroom and into your presence. Only you can heal this hurt. Only you can release me from the lie that I am *unlovable.*"

I read: *David shepherded them with integrity of heart: with skillful hands he led them* (Psalm78:72).

The Lord was asking me to trust him as a child would trust her father. This was no easy task, because I had been betrayed by my earthly father. In an attempt to guard my heart from God, I asked, "But what about the damage I have done to my husband, my children and my family while unconsciously protecting myself because of the terrible things that have been done to me?"

His firm but gentle answer came....

O afflicted city, lashed by storms and not comforted,
I will build you with stones of turquoise,
your foundations with sapphires.
I will make your battlements of rubies,
your gates of sparkling jewels,
and all your walls of precious stones.
All your sons will be taught by the LORD,
and great will be your children's peace.
In righteousness you will be established:
Tyranny will be far from you;
you will have nothing to fear.
Terror will be far removed;
it will not come near you.
If anyone does attack you, it will not be my doing;

whoever attacks you will surrender to you.
See, it is I who created the blacksmith
who fans the coals into flame
and forges a weapon fit for its work.
And it is I who have created the destroyer to work havoc;
no weapon forged against you will prevail,
and you will refute every tongue that accuses you.
This is the heritage of the servants of the LORD,
and this is their vindication from me,
declares the LORD (Isaiah 54:11-17).

He was proclaiming my vindication! He was saying I was cherished. He was calling me beautiful. He was affirming peace for my children. He was saying that I did not have to be afraid. He was declaring that I could be strong because of my heritage in Him. He was saying, "Come to me."

I took the first wobbly steps of a little child into believing that I could really trust him.

Reflecting on God's Light

Principle: *If I try to resolve my present conflict without finding healing for my past wounds, I will find, at best, only temporary relief. However, if I allow Jesus to heal my past, my present is redeemed!*

---

1. Think about it seriously. Can you honestly say that you trust Jesus to recognize and address your needs?

   _____

   _____

2. Are you willing to invest time and energy pursuing the Lord if it means you can be free of the wounds in your heart?

   _____

   _____

3. Is there a "bathroom" in your past? Are you willing to ask the Lord to heal your past wounds?

   _____

   _____

4. Have you developed life habits in response to abuse that seem to control you? (You want to feel and behave differently but you do not know how.)

_____

_____

_____

_____

5. What promises are found in the Isaiah 54:11-17 passage?

_____

_____

_____

_____

_____

_____

Chapter Seven

The Lord declares,
"Seek me and live..."
(Amos 5:4)

The Raging Storm

Then they cried out to the Lord in their trouble,
and he brought them out of their distress.
He stilled the storm to a whisper; the waves of
the sea were hushed. They were glad when
it grew calm, and he guided them
to their desired haven.

PSALM 107:28-30

I once bought a small plaque framed in blue with delicate flowers painted around the edges. The quote printed in the middle of the oval mat said, "Sometimes the Lord takes His child out of the raging storm, and sometimes He takes the raging storm out of his child." Over the next few months I had a sense of the Lord beginning to take the "raging storm" out of this child. One of my journal entries reads:

"I come this morning thanking you for the newness of heart you have given me. Satan continues to throw his darts and I still respond, but I think I am doing better. I find your peace more quickly. Thank you, Lord."

I was beginning to learn I could trust the Lord, and that trusting him brings peace.

In *The Three Battlegrounds*, Francis Frangipane writes,

> *In the battles of life, your peace is a weapon. Indeed, your confidence declares that you are not falling for the lies of the devil. You see, the first step toward having spiritual authority over the adversary is having peace in spite of your circumstances. When Jesus confronted the devil, He did not confront Satan with his emotions or fear. Knowing that the devil is a liar, He simply refused to be influenced by any other voice than God's. His peace overwhelmed Satan, His authority then shattered the lie, which sent demons fleeing.*[1]

Where do we find the kind of peace Frangipane is describing? Luke 8:24-25 says,

> *The disciples went and woke him, saying, "Master, Master, we're going to drown!" He got up and rebuked the wind and the raging waters; the storm subsided, and all was calm. "Where is your faith?" he asked his disciples.*

Why was Jesus asking *"Where is your faith?"* He might have been putting a finger on the pulse of their relationship with him. He was right there. Did they think he would allow them to die? The disciples understood their desperation to live, as do you and I. Perhaps they were trusting in his power, which they had seen, rather than in his love relationship with them, which they still did not fully comprehend.

I was reminded of a story I wrote several years ago about how we seek things to satisfy our needs and desires when we do not fully comprehend how much Jesus loves us. The fact that Jesus (and Jesus alone) can calm our internal storms is all too often lost in a raging sea of confusion and self-help. Here is the story:

Around daybreak, I was rudely awakened by a resounding "thud." You know—the kind that startles your foggy mind into wondering, "What was that?" As I brushed the mental cobwebs aside searching for a reasonable explanation, I thought, "The cardinal!" We had a pair of cardinals who came to the feeders off our back porch each day. They were mesmerizing! The male was bright crimson with a black face, red crest and an orange beak. He was always the perfect gentleman, coming to the feeder first to make sure things were safe for the female. He often sat patiently on an outer branch of the tree while she fed, then led the way as they retreated into the cedars. The bright red of a male cardinal splashed against a backdrop of dark green is a glorious sight! The female, not nearly so handsome, was a dusty brown with a dark crest and orange beak. She was a trusting and loyal mate, steady in her movements, rarely startled, and from her demeanor you could tell that she felt safe under the guardianship of her regal mate. Somehow, the word "submissive" came to mind.

So why was my reverie interrupted by these wonderful birds? The female had become entranced by the tall windows in our living room. She kept trying to fly through the window and into the house. She was very persistent. When this ritual began, she would fly into the window every thirty minutes or so. Sometimes it lasted for hours! I often wondered, "How foolish can you be, silly bird? You are bashing your beautiful head against an impenetrable window, and yet you persist as though your life depended on it! Even if you could get through, there is nothing good in here for you; no food, no freedom to fly, no protective mate. You are hurting yourself with this unrelenting behavior. Why? Why?"

That morning the Lord whispered in my ear, "How like you she is." Startled and appalled, I asked rather sarcastically, "How is that, Lord?" (Not a good move! I'm slowly learning never to ask the Lord for an explanation with such a flippant attitude. But I was still groggy and tired.) He brought to mind those times when I stubbornly pursued a piece of furniture (I am a sucker for antiques), just the right bedspread (to satisfy my sense of color and balance), or even a sensible pair of school shoes (a necessary item, right?) when there was really no money for these things. I'd just charge them. *Thump!* I saw those times when I had anxiously sought something I knew the Lord had promised me, not willing to wait for His perfect timing. *Thump!* I felt the pain my anger caused when someone was inconsiderate or had taken me for granted. *Thump!* I sensed the tension in my body caused by fretting and worrying about things over which I had no control. *Thump!* I remembered, sitting in front of the television watching mindless movies when I might have been enriching myself in the Word. *Thump!*

"Okay! Okay! I get the picture."

The Lord was telling me that antiques, bedspreads, shoes, friends, family and movies are "beyond the window." They are places that can trap and injure me and yet, like the cardinal, they are places I consistently pursue. Any "thing," person or emotion that takes my eyes off the Lord is dangerous. So why do I persist in this kind of head bashing? Why, indeed? I seek instant gratification. I feel as though I have rights and needs which ought to be fulfilled. I think I deserve to be healthy and happy. I am intent on having the necessities of life, as I see them, met.

The Lord declares *Seek me and live* (Amos 5:4). He says, *Woe to those who go down to Egypt for help, who rely on horses, who trust in the multitude and their chariots and in the strength of their horsemen, but do not look to the Holy One of Israel, or seek help from the LORD* (Isaiah 31:1).

I prayed, "Father, help me to remember that the necessary things of my life are in you alone before, like the cardinal, I thump myself to death.

Even back then, the Lord was gently leading me into a path of trusting Him!

In the book, *Come Away My Beloved*, Frances Roberts describes many beautiful promises the Lord uses to draw us to Himself.

Keep Your Face Toward the Sunrise

Behold, I have sent you out alone,
but I have gone ahead to prepare your way;
yes, through the darkness to bear a light.

I ask you only to follow me,
for I will surely lead you in a safe path,
  though dangers lurk on every hand.
Yes, I will be your protection.
I will be your comfort.
I will be your joy.
I will turn the bitter tear to sweet perfume.
By My Spirit, I will mend the broken heart,
I will pour warm fragrant oil into the deep wound.
For my heart is fused with your heart,
and in your grief, I am one with you.
Yes, I will fill the vacant place.
My arms shall hold you, and you will not fall.
My grace shall sustain you, and you will not faint.
My joy will fortify your spirit
even as a broken body is rejuvenated by a blood transfusion.
My smile shall dispel the shadows,
and My voice shall speak courage.
Yes, I will surely keep you, and you will not know fear.
You shall rest your foot upon the threshold of heaven.
I shall hide you in My pavilion.
You shall have My constant care.
I will not leave you for a moment.
I will keep you from despair;
I will deliver you from confusion.
When you are perplexed,
I will guide you in wisdom and in judgment.
By your light others shall be led out of the valley.
By your courage the weak shall be lifted up.
By your steadfastness he that wavers shall be stabilized.
Lo, the hour is upon you.
Do not look back.

Keep your face toward the sunrise,
for He shall rise fresh daily in your soul
with healing in His wings.[2]

The realization began to settle like a warm wool blanket. Not only was I desperate for the binding cords to be cut. I was also desperate for *him!* I would never be safe from the raging storm if I did not *fully* trust him to be in control!

I had to take the risk!

Chapter Seven

Reflecting on God's Light

1. Do you have peace in your heart, even in the midst of a raging storm in your life? Do you suffer from anxiety attacks? Insomnia? Nightmares?

   _____

   _____

2. Why is peace so important and how do we obtain it?

   _____

   _____

   _____

   _____

3. What is the significance of the story about the cardinal? What *things* do you use to try to fill the hole in your heart?

   _____

   _____

   _____

   _____

   _____

4. "Keep Your Face Toward the Sunrise" describes promises the Lord makes to us if we choose to trust him. List four promises that are important to you, today.

_____

_____

_____

_____

Chapter Eight

I remained silent—
hop, lunge, compensate.

The Crippled Crow

> *For there is a proper time and procedure for every matter, though a man's misery weighs heavily upon him.*
>
> ECCLESIASTES 8:6

Have you ever seen a crippled crow? There was one in our yard some time ago and the image of him hopping around stuck with me. He was missing a leg so his movements were very erratic: *hop, lunge forward, compensate*. His yellow eyes darted in their sockets, ever anxious to avoid danger. His feathers were mussed and ugly; after all, it is hard to preen when you are off balance. Can you visualize that crippled crow?

By the fall of the first year of my healing journey, that was how I was feeling. I had always tried to do the right thing, and going home for Christmas was one of those things. But I found myself caught up in a fierce struggle. I was beginning to experience some healing and freedom, but found the thought of returning "home" made me physically ill. I just could not do it! The guilt and anxiety raged. I was not able to keep my emotions balanced: *hop, lunge, compensate.*

I had talked to my mother and brother years before about having been molested, but they seemed to have forgotten! So I took a huge risk and wrote my mother a letter. I poured my heart into that letter. I asked the Lord to give me honest but gracious words. It was not an easy task because I needed her love and acceptance. I wrote that I had forgiven my father, and her, but my emotions were just too raw to be in that house for Christmas. I put the letter in the mail with extra postage and a prayer that it would be well received.

She responded in an angry, protective-of-Ann tone that set my heart spinning with expectation. By this time my father's condition had progressed to the point that he was on a feeding tube. In her anger, she threatened to go and rip it out. She said, "I remember that time in the bedroom. I asked him what was going on and he just laughed and said you were playing around. Did he rape you? You might forgive him, but I don't think I ever can!" I finally felt I had the protective guardianship of my mother. I was relieved and encouraged.

She was so upset that I suggested she seek counsel with her pastor. To my surprise, she did. We talked numerous times by phone and she finally seemed to find her balance again. Eventually, she asked if she should read the letter I had sent to be placed in my father's casket when he died. In an effort to reassure her I responded, "I don't care if you read it or not. I don't care what you do with it." As the words left my lips, I knew it was a lie. I did care, but I was basking like a child in her concern for me. I should have listened to the still small voice whispering words of caution in my ear. Instead, I was afraid that she would misunderstand my motives and withdraw her love, so I remained silent: *hop, lunge, compensate.*

I did not go home for Christmas.

Reflecting on God's Light

1. As you move along the road to healing, you may have to establish some new and difficult boundaries with family or friends. What might these boundaries include?

_____

_____

_____

_____

Example: *You were repeatedly abused by an older cousin when you were in elementary school. You are finally coming to terms with the reality of the abuse. You talk to your parents about the abuse. They express concern and accept your words as being reasonable and true. Yet, when you arrive at your parent's home for Thanksgiving dinner, the cousin is there—an invited guest.*

2. How would that situation make you feel?

_____

_____

_____

_____

3. What could you do and still express honor for God,
   your parents and yourself?

   _____

   _____

   _____

   _____

Chapter Nine

He was waiting for me there,
behind the fence.

The Fence and the Funeral

*Arise, come, my darling;
my beautiful one, come with me.*

SONG OF SOLOMON 2:13

There was a great time of intimacy and fellowship with the Lord throughout the winter, so I was surprised when I hit a dry spell in the spring. I was not anxious or fretting; things were just quiet for a while. I asked a friend to pray with me. As we prayed, all I could see in my mind's eye was a stack of old boards. It made no sense to me. As I continued to pray over a period of several weeks, I could see the Lord building a fence. He and I were on one side of the fence and the rest of the world was on the other side. We played and romped, I sat in his lap and he sang to me; we danced. It was as though I were a small child—his child. It was a heady feeling.

In June of that year, my father died in his sleep at the nursing home. I had lost any sense of connectedness to him over the past year. I felt I had already said my goodbyes. His passing brought only a final sigh of release. I gathered my immediate family around me and we headed home.

My mother and brother handled all of the arrangements. Things were under control. The casket had been left open with pictures taken over his lifetime displayed on an easel and propped inside the casket. Since my father was a World War II veteran, the casket was draped with an American flag. A Christian flag and an American Legion flag flanked each end.

I could manage only a cursory glance. The viewing of a dead body has always made me uncomfortable. So I simply stepped away to wait quietly while the rest of the family said their goodbyes. I vacillated between being distracted by well-wishers and trying not to throw up! My daughter edged next to me and whispered, "Mom, where is your letter?" I told her I assumed it was in the casket as I had asked. There was no reason to think my mother would not honor my wishes, yet a nagging fear began to grip my heart.

> ## Principle
>
> *The negative emotion I felt was a reflection of my past. The pain I felt matched the lies I had believed.* [1]

The morning of the funeral my mother called to remind us to be at the funeral home at 9:00 for the family gathering. That is when I asked her about my letter. She paused then replied, "I tore it up! I tore them both up and threw them in the garbage! You said you didn't care, so I thought it was alright for me to throw them away." I could barely breathe. I hung up the phone, dropped to the floor and began to keen like a wounded animal, howling softly with devastating grief.

That old familiar feeling of abandonment over-whelmed me. My throat was choked with gut-wrenching sobs surging up in waves. The pain was so intense I thought my skin would crack. She tore the letters up and threw them in the garbage. The things I had spent months preparing were nothing but trash. I felt as though she had chosen him over me, once again.

I rushed out of the motel room to find my husband in the parking lot—coffee in hand and a smile on his face. Recognizing my despair from a distance, he ush-ered me into a white plastic chair near the pool. He quaked as I shared my anguish then was very still for a while. Finally he said, "Ann, she just could not face it. She is still living in denial. I don't think she meant for this to hurt you even though it has. She just cannot deal with the truth and her own woundedness."

So I put on my "orange vest," pulled down my mask and survived the next few hours.

When I was finally home and able to talk with the Lord about my pain, he took me to the strangest place—2 Kings 25:27-30:

> *In the thirty-seventh year of the exile of Jehoiachin king of Judah, in the year Evil-Merodach became king of Babylon, he released Jehoiachin from prison on the twenty-seventh day of the twelfth month. He spoke kindly to him and gave him a seat of honor higher than those of the other kings who were with him in Babylon. So Jehoiachin put aside his prison clothes and for the*

rest of his life ate regularly at the king's table. Day by day the king gave Jehoiachin a regular allowance as long as he lived.

The Lord said, "Ann, you can either take off your smelly old prison clothes and come and join me at the king's table where I have made provision for you, or you can cling to the past (your expectations of understanding and acceptance by your family) and be miserable. The choice is yours."

The first step was to take off my prison clothes. *Put off your old self, which is being corrupted by its deceitful desires* (Ephesians 4:22). I was not wearing the black-and-white-striped uniform of a prisoner. Rather I wore a cloak of desires and expectations that focused on my family. I thought if they would not acknowledge the truth of my abuse that I could not be vindicated. I was holding them accountable. I needed their love and approval, which is not a bad thing, but I was putting that need ahead of my relationship with the Lord. Colossians 3:10 says, *Put on the new self, which is being renewed in knowledge in the image of its Creator.* The word for *put on* is *enduo*,[3] which literally means to be clothed or dressed by God himself. *To be made new in the attitude of your minds; and*

> ### Principle
>
> *When I acknowledged that the present situation was not the primary source of my pain, I opened a door that allowed me to examine the pain associated with my family's denial of the truth.*[2]

to put on the new self created, to be like God in true righteousness and holiness (Ephesians 4:23-24).

I began to see that the Lord had been preparing me for this difficult time. He was waiting for me there, behind the fence. I could see the banquet table set before me. I knew he would let me grieve my losses in his arms. I just had to give up my unholy desires and focus fully on him, knowing that he would meet my every need.

The immediate decision was easy. That tattered old cloak slid from my shoulders as I ran to Jesus, seeking his freedom. I made a choice that day, and Jesus is still fulfilling his promises to me. However, learning to really walk in his freedom has taken some time. Satan has tried repeatedly to distract me by twisting the words or actions of the ones I love into barbs that hurt me. It has taken me almost two years to learn to turn to the Lord as soon as the evil arrows of accusation fly.

I love my family, but their words and actions no longer turn my world upside down.

Chapter Nine

Reflecting on God's Light

> **Principle:** When I acknowledged that the present situation was not the primary source of my pain, I opened a door that allowed me to examine the pain associated with my family's denial of the truth.

1. If you had been in my place, what are some emotions you might have felt upon discovering that the letters had been thrown in the garbage?

   _____

   _____

   _____

2. What were some of the lies I had believed?

   _____

   _____

   _____

   _____

3. What "unrealistic" expectations had I placed on my family?

_____

_____

_____

_____

_____

4. What did the Lord ask me to do?

_____

_____

_____

_____

_____

Chapter Ten

Remember the wonders he has done.

The Meaning of "Forgive and Forget"

*May God himself, the God who makes everything holy
and whole, make you holy and whole, put you together—
spirit, soul, and body—and keep you fit for the coming of
our Master, Jesus Christ. The One who called you is
completely dependable. If he said it, he'll do it!*

1 THESSALONIANS 5:23,24 THE MESSAGE

T he message of *"forgive and forget"* is preached
from pulpits all over the world, and I am convinced it is a message from the pit of hell.
Forgive means to *"not hold accountable, to
pardon, to absolve, to release a debt."* To forget means
"to remove from memory, to overlook." However, our
brains are designed (by God) to develop and hold
memories. Those memories that are tied to some
physically or emotionally traumatic event have their
own specially designed neural pathways! It is
impossible to remove from memory such a thing.
The actual meaning of *"forgive and forget"* is *"forgive
and suppress."* This idea falls incredibly short of the
Lord's desire for our hearts and minds.

We ask the Lord to *take away our pain* rather than
heal our wounds. It is like taking aspirin for an
abscessed tooth. Eventually the aspirin wears off but

the abscess is still there. It is a vicious cycle, which keeps us bound and struggling to get free under our own power, rather than allowing the Lord to be the healer. Forgive and forget is a fantasy which can become, in a sense, idolatry. Ultimately we depend on *ourselves* to take away the ugly memories by suppressing them.

> *This is what the LORD says: "Your wound is incurable, your injury beyond healing. There is...no remedy for your sore, no healing for you...But I will restore your health and heal your wounds"* (Jeremiah 30:12,17).

> *He himself bore our sins in his body on the tree, so that we might die to sins and live for righteousness; by his wounds you have been healed* (1 Peter 2:24).

All through the Old Testament, the children of Israel were taught their oral history—stories of what the Lord had done to preserve them as a nation and a people. Whenever things got stressful or difficult (giants, floods, invading kings), they were always reminded of their history—their heritage in the Lord.

> *Look to the LORD and his strength; seek his face always. Remember the wonders he has done, his miracles, and the judgments he pronounced* (1 Chronicles 16:11-12).

> *I will remember the deeds of the LORD; yes, I will remember your miracles of long ago* (Psalm 77:11).

> *We have heard with our ears, O God; our fathers have*

told us what you did in their days, in days long ago (Psalm 44:1).

The memory of difficult times and the Lord's protection, intervention, and performing miracles on their behalf brought peace and a promise.

I believe the Lord wants the same thing for us. Let's not pretend the ugly things never happened. Let's expose the wounds. Let's allow the Lord to do his work of healing. Then let's *remember* his faithfulness, gentleness and power in the midst of those circumstances. His desire is for us to be the person he created us to be, as an individual, in the image of our Redeemer, Jesus Christ. His desire is for us to walk in righteousness. We will never get far along that journey until we allow the lies to be exposed, his truth to be revealed and our wounds to be *covered* by his blood.

> *Principle*
>
> *If I believe a lie, it might as well be true; the consequences will be the same! To be free of the lie, I must embrace and acknowledge it rather than deny it.*[1]

For Zion's sake I will not keep silent,
for Jerusalem's sake I will not remain quiet,
till her righteousness shines out like the dawn,
her salvation like a blazing torch.
The nations will see your righteousness,
and all kings your glory;
you will be called by a new name
that the mouth of the LORD will bestow.

You will be a crown of splendor in the LORD's hand,
a royal diadem in the hand of your God.
No longer will they call you Deserted,
or name your land Desolate.
But you will be called Hephzibah [my delight is in her],
and your land Beulah [married];
for the LORD will take delight in you,
and your land will be married.
As a young man marries a maiden,
so will your sons [Builder or God] *marry you;*
as a bridegroom rejoices over his bride,
so will your God rejoice over you (Isaiah 62:1-5).

On my fifty-sixth birthday my husband gave me an oval pendant that slides on a leather cord. Engraved on that piece are the letters "LPJ" as a reminder of the new name the Lord has given me— the Lord's Precious Jewel. It represents the Lord's covenant with me that I am a *royal diadem in the hand of my God.*

Forgive? Yes, yes, and amen! Forget? Never! Rather let us remember and rejoice in the Lord's incredible love for us and his great power to heal our wounds!

Reflecting on God's Light

> **Principle:** *If I believe a lie, it might as well be true; the consequences will be the same! To be free of the lie, I must embrace and acknowledge it rather than deny it.*

1. Have you ever been encouraged to forgive, forget and move on with your life? Were you able to do it? Why or why not?

_____

_____

_____

_____

_____

_____

2. When you forgive someone, you relinquish the debt they owe you. Forgiveness is for your release from the hold another has on your life. Is there a debt you need or want to release? What is it?

_____

_____

_____

_____

3. Can you find other scriptural examples of God's people being encouraged to *remember* the past? What was the purpose of remembering?

_____

_____

_____

_____

_____

_____

_____

_____

Chapter Eleven

*I was stunned, mystified
and then I was devastated...*

The Healing Journey

"For I know the plans I have for you," declares the LORD, "plans to prosper you and not to harm you, plans to give you hope and a future. Then you will call upon me and come and pray to me, and I will listen to you. You will seek me and find me when you seek me with all your heart. I will be found by you," declares the LORD, "and will bring you back from captivity."

JEREMIAH 29:11-14

"How do I get this healing?" you may be asking. "What do I do?"

I do not believe the Lord is restricted to only one way of getting us to the root of our problems. Sometimes he brings healing instantly through a miraculous intervention. If this type of healing brings immediate relief but not a long-term relationship with the Lord, however, it may be a quick fix rather than a cure. Sometimes he uses the Word alone. Sometimes he works through prayer ministry and counseling. Because of my own experiences, I would say that traditional cognitive therapy, where the emphasis lies with the counselor's expertise and your personal discipline rather than on the Lord as healer, is not enough by itself. Pray, look and listen. Be diligent. The Lord will bring you to the right place.

You who call on the LORD, give yourselves no rest, and give him no rest till he establishes Jerusalem (Isaiah 62:6-7). In other words, ask, ask, ask!

The healing journey, as I see it, is threefold:

○ the healing of a wound by the Lord,

○ the identification of sinful behavior that has become a life habit because of that wound,

○ recognition that it takes discipline to walk in freedom because Satan is still here and we are still human.

One morning during my quiet time, the Lord took me on just such a journey. I was reading in the book of Isaiah 54:4-5:

Do not be afraid; you will not suffer shame. Do not fear disgrace; you will not be humiliated. You will forget the shame of your youth and remember no more the reproach of your widowhood (abandonment).

(His assurance that the wounds of my youth are being healed)

For your Maker is your husband–the LORD Almighty is his name—the Holy One of Israel is your Redeemer; he is called the God of all the earth.

(The promise of his protection)

The LORD will call you back as if you were a wife (a

child) deserted and distressed in spirit–a wife who married young, only to be rejected," says your God.

(The promise of his redemption—he will fight for me!)

"For a brief moment I abandoned you, but with deep compassion I will bring you back. In a surge of anger I hid my face from you for a moment, but with everlasting kindness I will have compassion on you," says the LORD your Redeemer.

Whoa! Wait a minute, Lord. Why are you angry with me? I am the one who was injured! I am the one who was abandoned! I was the victim! Why would you be angry with *me?*

He answered, "Even though you were wronged and have acted out of your pain, your responses of anger and control are not righteous responses. Likewise, when you worry about how your family will react or how the truth of who you are in me might impact them, you are putting them on my throne!"

I was stunned, mystified and then I was devastated that the Lord was displeased or angry with my behavior. I felt confused, yet again.

My heart groaned!

How long must I wrestle with my thoughts and every day have sorrow in my heart? How long will my enemy triumph over me? Look on me and answer, O LORD my God. Give light to my eyes, or I will sleep in death (Psalm 13:2).

I began to scour the Word for cross-references and explanations.

First I read Psalm 7:11, which says, *God is a righteous judge, a God who expresses his wrath every day.* The note in the NIV says, "God's judgments are not kept in store for some future day." Then I went to Psalm 2:5 cross-referencing the word *anger*: *Then he rebukes them in his anger and terrifies them in his wrath.* Note: "God's anger is always an expression of his righteousness."

My behavior was not righteous, no matter how I learned it, and he wanted me to change.

I then followed the cross-references to Isaiah 57:16, *I will not accuse forever, nor will I always be angry, for then the spirit of man will grow faint before me—the breath of man that I have created.* God understood my limitations and had compassion on me.

I could focus on learning how to be righteous (right with God) or I could focus on his anger. We all have that choice. Focusing on his anger keeps us a victim. That was certainly not where I wanted to be. I had experienced a taste of freedom and I intended to have more. So again I came to him clamoring like a child, "You have the blueprints. Make me right, Lord."

Note: Being made aware of his anger was a good thing because it sent me scurrying through the scriptures to find the reason. When we see things we do not understand, using the notes and cross references is always a good idea. There are also many helps, such as dictionaries and commentaries, which can enhance our understanding of the Word.

At my invitation, the Lord was stepping in to expose and heal my wounds. He was identifying my sinful life habits and showing me how to change them. Finally came my part, the "discipline" steps in the healing journey. It was not easy. In fact, I am still working on it! Discipline, choosing to walk and live in freedom, takes time, energy and attention to the Holy Spirit.

My anger is one area of, shall we say, continual learning. When I find myself getting agitated because I have been ignored or misunderstood, I begin looking for the Lord (most of the time). I might ask, "Lord, is this person really being rude or are we dealing with my own insecurities here? Have I somehow bumped into their painful wounds? How should I respond, Lord?" I wait and listen. I rarely speak unless I have his permission. I am diligent to speak only the words he gives me, sometimes with a graciousness that surprises even me. It is a battle, however, because Satan would like to lure me into abandoning my trust in my heavenly Father.

I spend time in the Word and reading, not because I ought to but because I want to. I seek out Christian friends for accountability. I pray for those who hurt me, because I know there is a neediness in them that was once so strong in me. I look at them with new eyes. I have long talks with my husband. Our relationship is more intimate because I no longer look to him to solve my problems. He can't. He is not God. I am less intense because I have greater freedom to become the person God created me to be. My relationship with my Lord is deeply personal. I have discovered that discipline can be a privilege and a joy when it brings us into God's righteousness. As Dallas Willard often says, "The rest just falls away."[1]

When I came across this verse in the book of Esther where King Xerxes was putting Queen Vashti away because she ignored his command, I had to smile.

> *Then when the king's edict is proclaimed throughout all his vast realm, all the women will respect their husbands, from the least to the greatest* (Esther 1:20).

The men making this decision might have been nobles, but they just didn't get it! Respect and trust are not the result of edicts but of relationship. In trusting, loving relationships we are willing to listen and bend because we know the other person has our very best at heart. An attempt to legislate respect is foreign to the nature of God. Jesus died for me! He gave everything to restore my relationship with the Father, and in my finite way I love him for that incredible gift.

The Lord also knows what our perfect image looks like and in his sovereignty is conscientious about drawing us into that image. We will never completely attain perfection until the "Day of Redemption" because we live in a fallen world—Satan and our sin nature. However, in *My Utmost For His Highest* Oswald Chambers wrote,

> *Whenever God's will is in complete control, He removes all pressure. And when we deliberately choose to obey*

Him, He will reach to the remotest star and to the ends of the Earth to assist us with all of His mighty power.[2]

I can live with that!!

Chapter Eleven

Reflecting on God's Light

1. Are the steps of the healing journey expressed in this chapter different from the things you have been told in the past? How?

_____

_____

_____

_____

2. What are some "helps" you might use when reading the scriptures?

_____

_____

_____

_____

3. Why do you think God expressed anger toward my *behavior?*

_____

_____

_____

_____

Chapter Twelve

It's time, Ann.
Let's get to the root of your fear.

You Want Bad? I'll Show You Bad.

I do not understand what I do. For what I want to do I do not do, but what I hate I do.

ROMANS 7:15

Over the years I developed a habit of being critical of anyone who threatened me emotionally or physically. I was really good at making light of those who caused me to feel uncomfortable. But the Lord was not honored by me criticizing someone else. He said, "Ann, you do this out of *fear*. With me there is nothing to fear. Will you trust me?" Again, he was offering me the chance for greater freedom.

But this time God was taking me into some uncharted territory. In the previous chapters I talked about my suppressed memories—the ones I chose not to acknowledge because I did not know how to deal with them. Counselors had given me strategies for keeping things under control, but until I asked the Lord for deep healing I still carried those memories around like old dirty baggage in a designer suitcase.

Even though I had already experienced a measure of healing, there was a growing awareness that more "circumcision" was needed in order for the shield around my hidden pain to be completely removed.

Dan and I were serving as facilitators for a conference called The Potter's Institute. The focus of the conference was healing the wounds of the heart. Dan is an accomplished potter and is able to bring the imagery of "the potter and the clay" to life by demonstrating the stages of making a pot on the wheel. Following the demonstration, we were asked to shape a lump of clay into the image of our hearts. As I began to pray, the Lord spoke to me, "Ann, there is a pocket of fear and sin that you are still holding on to. It is unbelief. Let me have it. You can trust me." So I molded my clay heart with a shield, like an eyelid partially closed, and I laid it on the potter's wheel. I asked the Lord to show me the root of this critical spirit. As always, he was faithful.

A week or so after the conference, I was reading Psalm 15 as part of my morning quiet time.

LORD, who may dwell in your sanctuary?
Who may live on your holy hill?
He whose walk is blameless
and who does what is righteous,
who speaks the truth with his heart
and has no slander on his tongue,
who does his neighbor no wrong
and casts no slur on his fellowman,
who despises a vile man
but honors those who fear the LORD,

who keeps his oath,
even when it hurts,
who lends his money without usury
and does not accept a bribe against the innocent.
He who does these things
will never be shaken (Psalm 15).

The word *slur* rattled something within me.

After reading this passage several times, the words "You want bad? I'll show you bad!" began to swirl around in my mind. I wasn't sure where they had come from, but they struck cold fear in my heart! I prayed, "Lord, what is the meaning of this?" The Lord answered, "It's time, Ann. Let's get to the root of your fear."

I was alone in my living room. After a few minutes of prayer I began to shake all over, crying and cringing. My breasts felt strange and I got sick at my stomach. The words and feelings were very vivid! There was a confusion of light and dark, but as I prayed the image in my mind became clear. My father and I were in the church yard. He had taken me outside because I had been a "bad" girl. I could see him pinching and twisting my nipples and whispering angrily, "You want bad? I'll show you bad!"

Principle

The pain I felt was not coming from the memory of the event, but rather from interpretation I had given the event: "If I was bad, I would be sexually abused."[1]

I cried and cried, overwhelmed with feelings of shame. I was sitting in my favorite chair, curving my shoulders as though to protect myself. I felt as though a curse had been placed on my life as a one-year-old child, that if I were "bad" I would be punished—sexually abused. It was my father's way of maintaining control. He was a deeply wounded man.

What did that have to do with my critical spirit? Was I struggling with a spiritual curse or was it learned behavior? I am not certain. In any case, I had been using that same mentality—"You want bad? I'll show you bad!" I was using a bad word, a "slur," to put people in their place. I was afraid someone's actions or words would hurt me, so I became critical in order to maintain control and push them away. The wretchedness of it made me ill! My attempts to control those around me by using words of criticism were just as unrighteous as my father's attempts to control my behavior by instilling fear through sexual abuse. Once again, I fell on my face before the Father asking for *healing* and then *forgiveness*.

> *Principle*
>
> *In the midst of darkness I came to realize how utterly bound I was to the lie I believed and how helpless I was in overcoming its debilitating grip on my life.*[2]

Satan stepped up immediately whispering: "This could not have really happened." "In the church-yard? Oh come on!" "You are imagining things." "After all, you *were* a bad girl. There are stories." "One-year-olds are not able to remember this way." He *lied*. This was my memory, my experience, my healing and, by God's grace, my victory.

Recent brain-based research indicates that the brain is building memories even in the womb. Much of the research emphasizes that memory is not totally predictable. Blanket descriptions do not always apply. The neural pathways that are established when we experience trauma bypass the traditional mode of making memories such as learning our ABC's or multiplication tables. Trauma sears memories into place quickly, immediately. Trauma is defined by the mind of the individual. It might result from something as simple as feeling totally isolated because someone laughed at you to being locked in a dark closet. Our feelings and emotions are the key.

If we are not able to make a connection between the trauma and a reasonable explanation, our brain may put the memory into a box; not a box with a pigeonhole, but a closed box. In psychological terms these would be called "repressed" memories. In those memories where we become the person watching from the outside rather than the person involved in what is taking place (becoming the "fly on the wall," so to speak) the term is *dissociation*.

The Lord was taking me into the "uncharted territory" of repressed memories. When our memories seem beyond reason, the logical questions are, "Did you imagine that?" "Did you make it up?" Remember that repressed memories are often trauma-based. They record a terribly painful situation or circumstance. People do not "make up" incredibly painful circumstances and then stuff them away as repressed memories. If they "make up" painful circumstances, it is usually for the purpose of drawing attention to themselves. Repressed memories are the kind no one wants to talk about! Therein lies the difference.

A root of fear related to physical pain was established in my memory at the tender age of one. I believe the Lord was showing me that my trauma, that day in the churchyard, began to form the fear-based root of my critical spirit. Years later, during my quiet time in my living room, he was showing me the truth. Out of fear I pushed people away through criticism. It had nothing to do with my head, but everything to do with my wounded heart.

You do not support the root, but the root supports you (Romans 11:18).

Principle

No one, including myself, was capable of talking me out of the lie, but I was set free when I heard the truth from the one who is Truth, Jesus Christ.[3]

Chapter Twelve

Reflecting on God's Light

> **Principle:** *In the midst of darkness I came to realize how utterly bound I was to the lie I believed and how helpless I was in overcoming its debilitating grip on my life.*

1. Is there a behavior in your life that you keep *working* to change, but it never seems to get any better or change completely?

_____

_____

_____

_____

2. Ask the Lord to show you the root of that behavior. Is it rooted in a lie?

_____

_____

_____

_____

> **Principle:** *No one, including myself, was capable of talking me out of the lie, but I was set free when I heard the truth from the one who is Truth, Jesus Christ.*

3. We look at life through the grid of the "lies we believe." When the lies are removed and replaced with God's truth, our minds are changed, transformed and renewed.

   For though we walk in the flesh, we do not war according to the flesh, for the weapons of our warfare are not of the flesh, but divinely powerful for the destruction of fortresses. We are destroying speculations and every lofty thing raised up against the knowledge of God, and we are taking every thought captive to the obedience of Christ (2 Corinthians 10:3-6 NASB).

4. According to this principle, what can change, transform or renew our minds? Is that true to your experience?

_____

_____

_____

_____

_____

Chapter Thirteen

I have given you the heart of a lion.
I will preserve you.

The Basin, Then the Bedroom

Whoever touches you touches the apple of his eye–I will surely raise my hand against them so that their slaves will plunder them. Then you will know that the LORD Almighty has sent me.

JEREMIAH 2:8-9

The Lord is always so gracious and gentle in that he only takes me as far as I can stand to go. I do not go for counseling or prayer ministry once a week or once a month. I seek help when my emotions become painful and I know he is leading me to examine another memory. After that last memory emerged, my father's words kept spinning around in my head, "You want bad? I'll show you bad!" I would physically shudder to shake off the feeling that came with them. I was not afraid, just agitated. I sought the assistance of a prayer minister to help me pray.

As we began to pray, the first memory the Lord led me into was of my great-grandparents' house in the country. There was a tall picket fence with a gate in the middle. I could see the tree where the produce scale hung near the steps to the front porch. There was emotional pain associated with this memory. I went back to the time when I dropped the washbasin off the gallery and it broke. The washbasin was a large flowered bowl which had been, at one time, part of a bowl and pitcher set. It was very old. The gallery was a long board which hung out over the edge of the porch. When the men came in from the fields they would use the basin and water from a bucket to wash their hands. There was no running water.

Paw had cautioned me not to try to empty the basin by myself. I was so small that I had to stand on a railing just to reach the bowl. Wanting to be a big girl, I tried it anyway. The basin slipped from my tiny hands, crashing into the bed of red and yellow cannas below. Paw was so angry! I was so embarrassed. I had made a mistake. I had disappointed and upset my great-grandfather, a man I worshiped.

It was awful. My heart was broken—like the basin. As I continued to watch the image develop, the Lord came through the gate. He walked in among the cannas and started picking up the shattered pieces. Looking up at me, a little girl hanging off the edge of the gallery with tears in her eyes, He smiled—such a beautiful, laughing smile. He said, "Ann, it is okay. It is just an old bowl." Peace flooded my heart.

After a while a second memory began to emerge. I saw myself in a bedroom in that same house. It was my great-uncle's room. I had always been fascinated by the razor strap that hung by the dresser—scary stories had been told about that razor strap. Then there was the pretty bed. It had an iron frame with brass knobs attached to the sculpted white metal.

But I wasn't supposed to be in that room

My grandmother had always accused me of "plundering." To plunder means to take something as the spoils of war. Jeremiah 30:16 says, *But all who devour you will be devoured; all your enemies will go into exile. Those who plunder you will be plundered; all who make spoil of you I will despoil.* I was a four-year-old child. I was curious; I was not plundering. I wasn't doing anything wrong, but I wasn't supposed to be in that room.

I became aware of physical sensations known as "body memories." They began to intensify. I began rubbing my hand across my forehead because it felt as though my head was being pressed against something. There was pain across the back of my neck and I found it difficult to breathe. I was sick at my stomach and flailing my arms and legs. I had a sense of being held down with my face against the mattress of the pretty white bed. There was anal pain. I was being sodomized by two drunken men. They were laughing at me. There was a red rag (probably a bandana) stuffed in my mouth so no one could hear my screams.

Satan's lies began to flow. "You are worthless." "No one cares that you are being hurt." "You are helpless." "You can't say a word!" "Your fighting back means nothing at all."

The Lord answered the lies in that memory with his truth. He said, "Ann, I have given you the *heart of a lion!* You are not worthless. You are a fighter and I have

> *Principle*
>
> *I was emotionally bound to the lies.*[1]

things to say through you that are important. I will preserve you." He was all around me—at the side of the bed hovering as though to protect me, at the foot of the bed angry and pushing them away, in the dark corner filling it with light and then drawing the blanket as a covering over me. After a time with the Lord I was calm. I could breathe again and the image began to fade. I prayed:

Dear Lord, help me to be your vessel. You have placed this heart in me—even at the age of four. May it beat strongly with your Spirit, your compassion, your boldness, Your love. Thank you, Lord, for showing me the truth of who I am—once again. Satan has tried to destroy me, but you have been faithful. Thank you, Jesus.

Your daughter,
Ann

But this is what the LORD says:
"Yes, captives will be taken from warriors,
and plunder retrieved from the fierce;
I will contend with those who contend with you,
and your children I will save.
I will make your oppressors eat their own flesh;
they will be drunk on their own blood, as with wine.
Then all mankind will know
that I, the LORD, am your Savior,
your Redeemer, the Mighty One of Jacob"
(Isaiah 49:25-26).

I was free only when I heard the truth from the One who is Truth, Jesus Christ.

Chapter Thirteen

Reflecting on God's Light

Principle: *I was emotionally bound to the lies.*

---

1. Why do you think this became a repressed memory for me?

_____

_____

_____

_____

2. Why would a four-year-old believe Satan's lies?

_____

_____

_____

_____

3. Record the lies that were spoken when I was four
   and God's truths I received fifty years later:

SATAN'S LIES	GOD'S TRUTHS

4. I was only free when _____

_____

Chapter Fourteen

Process time is important and
conversation with the Lord
is imperative.

Naked and Alone

"Today I have made you a fortified city, an iron pillar and a bronze wall to stand against the whole land...They will fight against you but will not overcome you, for I am with you and will rescue you," declares the LORD.

JEREMIAH 1:18-19

The Lord uses present-day frustrations, anxieties and fears to help expose the past wounds in our lives that need to be healed. He uses our emotions to draw us to Him. At one point I had been struggling with a number of issues that seemed to have a common denominator. I was feeling "outside the circle" with family and friends. I felt *alone.* People seemed to be either not listening or ignoring my concerns. Even innocent occurrences that hinted at leaving me out escalated my pain. In my own eyes I was being unreasonable, but the pain was very real. I could not seem to get past it. I was desperate for relief.

Even though the timing was off (my husband was preparing for a wedding and I was falling apart), I began to seek the Lord. The wedding was out of town, so we were staying at a motel. As I rocked on the bed, eyes closed and praying, I began to feel a deep sadness. The Lord was taking me to another repressed memory. There was an orange glow. I could see, in my mind's eye, the sun rising. I was in the sheep-shearing barn at my great-grandfather's farm. As the sunlight penetrated the darkness, I could see myself. I was lying atop a pile of dusty wool in one of the wool bins (a wooden stall where the wool was tossed after being sheared from the sheep). I was curled in the fetal position, asleep, with a little turquoise dress at my feet. I was five years old, naked and alone.

My pain turned to hysteria. How could someone dump me on a pile of wool like a piece of worthless trash? Why was I there? It was obvious that I had been used, but I could not even consider it for a while. I was totally undone. Everyone around me was busy in preparation for the big day. I didn't want to steal my husband's focus but I was too hysterical to appear in public. There was no one to talk to. I was alone, alone, alone.

Again I prayed, "Lord, where were you?" I peered down to see him sitting beside me on the wool and covering me with a blanket, his quiet countenance calming my heart. Eventually I saw myself walking out of that barn, in my turquoise dress, hand in hand with Jesus. With this kind of traumatic memory, there is no instant release. Process time is

> **Principle**
>
> *In this hopeless, helpless state I was able to receive his healing touch. With his touch came peace.*[1]

important and conversation with the Lord is imperative. The adrenalin rush is real and it takes time to recover both physically and emotionally. But I knew he was there and he had covered me—things were going to be all right.

When we arrived home, I sought out a friend who does prayer ministry. I needed to know how I had gotten there—in that wool bin. Part of that barn was an old garage. The memory started there. I could see the slatted walls, feel the gravel on the dirt floor grinding into my knees and smell the musty oil. It was night. There was a kerosene lantern glowing in one corner, casting giant shadows on the walls. Men were drunk and laughing. I was being forced to perform oral sex for one of them. I gagged, threatening to throw up. My mind reeled. I collapsed—used up. I do not remember being moved from the garage to the wool bin. The next thing I do remember is seeing the sunrise.

Does the Lord really know about such evil? Of course He does!

> Their cobwebs are useless for clothing;
> they cannot cover themselves with what they make.
> Their deeds are evil deeds,
> and acts of violence are in their hands.
> Their feet rush into sin;
> they are swift to shed innocent blood.
> Their thoughts are evil thoughts;
> ruin and destruction mark their ways.
> The way of peace they do not know;
> there is no justice in their paths.

They have turned them into crooked roads;
no one who walks in them will know peace
(Isaiah 59:6-8).

How long will the wicked, O LORD,
how long will the wicked be jubilant?
They pour out arrogant words;
all the evildoers are full of boasting.
They crush your people, O LORD ;
they oppress your inheritance.
They slay the widow and the alien;
they murder the fatherless.
They say, "The LORD does not see;
the God of Jacob pays no heed" (Psalm 94:3-7).

Who will rise up for me against the wicked?
Who will take a stand for me against evildoers?
Unless the LORD had given me help,
I would soon have dwelt in the silence of death.
When I said, "My foot is slipping,"
your love, O LORD, supported me.
When anxiety was great within me,
your consolation brought joy to my soul
(Psalm 94:16-19).

Except for the Lord's covering and protection in the midst of those times, I am convinced I would have died—naked and alone.

Reflecting on God's Light

Principle: In this hopeless, helpless state I was able to receive His healing touch. With his touch came peace.

Helpless—five years old

Hopeless—confused and brutalized

His Touch

- He covered my naked body with a blanket.
- He sat with me and waited.
- He dressed me.
- He held my hand and walked with me to a place of safety.
- He preserved my life!

Will you allow him to touch and heal *your* wounded heart?

Chapter Fifteen

I was alone, a "bother."

The Return of the Prodigal Son

Naked I came from my mother's womb,
and naked I will depart.

JOB 1:21

O ddly enough, this memory was revealed around Mother's Day two years after the beginning of my deep healing journey. I remember because we had conducted a retreat with several other couples and our host gave all of the ladies magnificent bouquets for Mother's Day. The setting was lovely and relaxed, but the teaching was intense. The word *bother* began to stir around in my head during that weekend and I did not seem to be able to make it go away. For me, at least, this is a sure sign that I need to spend some time alone with the Lord.

The following week I sought a friend and prayer minister. As I focused on that word *bother*, the Lord began to direct me to a memory. I was thrashing about, but seemed trapped. There were muted colors of reddish-orange, gray and black. I could not see anything clearly. There was a suffocating pressure all around me and I was nauseous. It was the strangest feeling I had ever sensed and it continued for a long time. I was afraid. I felt pain on the front and back of my head. I really did not understand what was happening until there was suddenly a blinding light, and I was shivering. My memory was about being born! (Now I am a practical, analytical person so this was a real stretch for me. But the Lord had brought me there, so he must have had a purpose.)

The light was intense and the images fuzzy. I was in the fetal position, cold and naked. No one came for me. Two hands were holding me out in front of them, but not cuddling me or wrapping me in a blanket. I was alone, a "bother." Whether that "feeling" came from the trauma of being born or whether it was conveyed to me in the womb, I honestly cannot say. The circumstances leading up to my birth were tenuous, at best. Even then, Satan was speaking lies.

My father was a World War II veteran, having recently returned home from overseas. He was a rakish young man of twenty-six. My mother was only sixteen and a still in high school. I do not know how they got together, but she had to drop out of school when she became pregnant. They were married in May. I was born in January. They lived in a small town so the rumors must have been rampant, the shame intense. My mother might possibly have sought an abortion and my life been snuffed out before it really began. I am eternally thankful that she did not choose that path. Satan would have been delighted.

There are many layers to this story, but I want to focus on that word *bother*. Henri Nouwen wrote an incredibly wonderful book entitled *The Return of the Prodigal Son*. This book details his study of Rembrandt's exquisite, dusky painting by the same title. As he talks about the prodigal preparing to return to his father's house, he muses that the thoughts in the young man's heart might have run along these lines: "My heart grows heavy. My body is filled with sorrows. My life loses meaning. I have become a lost soul. I will return home." But on the way home the son prepares this scenario: "Father, I have sinned against heaven and against you; I no longer deserve to be called your son; treat me as one of your hired men."[1]

(In other words, I have been a great "bother." Forgive me as much as you can.)

Nouwen goes on to say, "Receiving forgiveness requires a total willingness to let God be God and do all the healing, restoring and renewing. As long as I want to do even a part of that myself, I end up with partial solutions, such as becoming a hired servant. As a hired servant, I can still keep my distance, still revolt, reject, strike, run away, or complain about my pay. As the beloved son, I have to claim my full identity and begin preparing myself to become like the father."[2]

(If I hold on to anything or anyone other than Jesus Christ, if I hold back even one area of my life, then I am rejecting the opportunity to be his son or daughter.)

"Jesus makes it clear that the way to God is the same as the way to new childhood. 'Unless you turn and become like little children you will never enter the Kingdom of Heaven.' Jesus does not ask me to remain a child but to become one. Becoming a child is living *toward a second innocence*; not the innocence of the newborn infant, but the innocence that is reached *through conscious choices*."[3] (emphasis added)

(If I do not come to the Father with the unhindered expectation of an innocent little child and a willingness to allow him to touch me and heal me and teach me, then I will miss the blessing of life. Are you willing?)

"And as I reach home and feel the embrace of my Father, I will realize that not only heaven will be mine to claim, but the earth as well will become my inheritance, a place where I can live in freedom without obsessions and compulsions."[4]

(Have you received that freedom from Jesus Christ? If not, he is drawing you to himself even in this moment. Run to him! Do not allow the sense of being a "bother" keep you from him.)

"Isn't the little child poor, gentle, and pure of heart? Isn't the little child weeping in response to every little pain? And what of Jesus himself, the Word of God who became flesh, dwelt for nine months in Mary's womb, and came into this world as a little child worshiped by shepherds from close by and by wise men from far away? The eternal Son became a child so that I might become a child again and so re-enter with him into the "Kingdom of the Father."[5]

"I am touching here the mystery that Jesus himself became the prodigal son for our sake. He left the house of his heavenly Father, came to a foreign country, gave away all that he had, and returned through his cross to his Father's home. All of this he did, not as a rebellious son, but as the obedient son, sent out to bring home all the lost children of God."[6]

(You are not a "bother." You are His beloved child. He has loved you from before the time you were formed in the womb. He has a wonderful, life-giving plan for you. He loves you beyond your ability to imagine. Don't push him away because you have been hurt or betrayed by those you should have been able to trust. Let him love you.)

In my memory, Jesus *did* come for me the day I was born. He wrapped me in a cottony soft blanket and cooed and cuddled me as his precious child. He said he was delighted with me. He wants to do the same for you. Will you surrender your life to Him?

Be brave enough to begin "looking with new eyes." Give yourself to him and acknowledge him as your Savior.

Chapter Fifteen

Reflecting on God's Light

1. Have you ever felt as though you were a "bother?"

_____

_____

_____

2. Do you approach God with the same timid mindset as the prodigal as he returned home: "Forgive me as much as you can?" If so, what does that say about your perspective of God?

_____

_____

_____

_____

3. Nouwen addresses the mystery of becoming a child again by saying we can live "toward a second innocence." What does that mean?

_____

_____

_____

_____

4. Have you accepted God's gift of life through Jesus
   Christ? If not, invite him into your heart right now!

Chapter Sixteen

*Our stiff-necked unbelief
can become our idol.*

Yes, but...

If any of you lacks wisdom, he should ask God, who gives generously to all without finding fault, and it will be given to him. But when he asks, he must believe and not doubt, because he who doubts is like a wave of the sea, blown and tossed by the wind.

JAMES 1:5-6

You may be thinking just that...

- ○ "Yes, but you don't know my pain." *He himself bore our sins in his body on the tree, so that we might die to sins and live for righteousness; by his wounds you have been healed* (1 Peter 2:24).

○ "Yes, but this can't be fixed. It is beyond repair." *It is for freedom that Christ has set us free. Stand firm, then, and do not let yourselves be burdened again by a yoke of slavery* (Galatians 5:1). *Take off the grave clothes and let him go* (John 11:44, speaking of Lazarus).

○ "Yes, but they will hurt me or kill me." *No weapon forged against you will prevail, and you will refute every tongue that accuses you* (Isaiah 54:17).

❍ "Yes, but I do not have a compassionate, supporting spouse." *My soul finds rest in God alone; my salvation comes from him. He alone is my rock and my salvation; he is my fortress, I will never be shaken* (Psalm 62:1-2).

As stated earlier, the devastating statistics given by Dan Allender are that at least 52 percent of all women and 33 percent of all men have experienced some form of sexual abuse by the age of eighteen. The estimates given by T.D. Jakes run even higher. If you are a woman who has been sexually abused, you are not alone. Indeed, you are part of the majority. There is no glory in this. It is heartbreaking! I sat one morning listing the names of women I have met in the last three years who suffered sexual abuse as children. In a few short minutes I had written down thirty-two names of women ranging in age from twelve to seventy-five! Most of those women are still bound in fear and shame. They either do not know or are just beginning to learn about the freedom Christ is offering them. Satan would say to you, "You are the only one." *He is a liar!*

I was listening to a tape recently by Malcolm Smith about victims and martyrs. At one point he was talking about Christ having experienced the same pain that we have experienced. When he said something about Jesus having experienced sexual abuse, I sat up and listened harder. He said that Jesus experienced sexual abuse because he hung on that cross not draped in a loin cloth, but naked. He was taunted, jeered at and spit upon in his nakedness. My skin crawled. My mind flashed back to *my* "most vulnerable moment" and in my heart I had to agree. Jesus was sexually abused. He suffered that for me... and you. He knows our pain. *For what the law was powerless to do in that it was weakened by the sinful nature, God did by sending his own Son in the likeness of sinful man to be a sin offering* (Romans 8:3).

Our "Yes, but..." responses are impotent. Our stiff-necked unbelief can become our idol, that sense of being personally in control. We can adopt the mindset of the prodigal to become a servant and hold on to our misery, *or* we can lay it at the foot of the cross beneath the naked broken body of Jesus and allow his blood to begin to cover us. He wants to teach us how to live, not just suffer well. He wants us to be as spiritually and emotionally free as little children.

His desire is for our very best. Our names are carved on the palms of His hands. He calls us "beloved"! He carries us on his strong back. He is our Abba, Father. *Let the beloved of the LORD rest secure in him, for he shields him all day long, and the one the LORD loves rests between his shoulders* (Deuteronomy 33:12).

In *Waking the Dead,* John Eldredge quotes Nelson Mandela as saying,

Our deepest fear is not that we are inadequate. Our deepest fear is that we are powerful beyond measure. It is our light, not our darkness, that most frightens us. We ask ourselves, "Who am I to be brilliant, gorgeous, talented and fabulous?" Actually, who are you not to be?

You are a child of God. Your playing small doesn't serve the world. There's nothing enlightened about shrinking so that other people won't feel insecure around you. We were born to manifest the glory of God that is within us...And as we let our own light shine, we unconsciously give other people permission to do the same. As we are liberated from our own fear, our presence automatically liberates others. [1]

There are no social programs adequate to stem the tide of sexual abuse, no legislation to make it stop. It is epidemic. But you and I have the power through Jesus Christ to become liberated from the effect it has had on our lives. As we are liberated, our presence will automatically liberate others to seek from him what they see in us.

One of my greatest joys is to sit across the table from a woman, hear her speak cautiously, tentatively about her abuse and be able to say, "I know. I have been there." I watch as the shoulders drop, the face relaxes, the tears glisten and the shame begins to slide away. A bond of understanding begins to develop because of her courage and the thing the Lord is doing in our lives. In that moment, with that one woman, all of my pain and suffering become worth it.

Praise be to the God and Father of our Lord Jesus Christ, the Father of compassion and the God of all comfort, who comforts us in all our troubles, so that we can comfort those in any trouble with the comfort we ourselves have received from God. For just as the sufferings

*of Christ flow over into our lives, so also through Christ
our comfort overflows* (2 Corinthians 1:3-7).

In *The Message* it reads like this:

*All praise to the God and Father of our Master, Jesus the
Messiah! Father of all mercy! God of all healing
counsel! He comes alongside us when we go through
hard times, and before you know it, he brings us alongside someone else who is going through hard times so
that we can be there for that person just as God was
there for us. We have plenty of hard times that come
from following the Messiah, but no more so than the
good times of his healing comfort—we get a full measure of that, too* (2 Corinthians 1:3-7).

It seems that every week I meet a woman who
has suffered sexual abuse. The Lord gives me the
great privilege of ministering his grace to these
women in some small way. It is a course he has set
before me. If he invites you, would you be willing to
join me—right where you live? You don't have to
write a book or direct a women's ministry or teach a
Bible study or go out looking for women with whom
to share your story. Those are wonderful things if the
Lord directs you to them. All you really have to do is
be available, listen to the prompting of the Holy
Spirit and then do as he says. It sounds simple but
takes courage, surrender and commitment.

The Lord has a plan for my life. I do not yet know
everything that encompasses, but in the midst of the
abuse he gave me the "heart of a lion" and "words to

speak." He called me beautiful, his beloved, his "precious jewel." He protected me. He came for me. And now he is taking me on an exciting adventure. I am free to be the person he created me to be. He preserved my life for this purpose.

He has preserved your life, as well.

Reflecting on God's Light

1. What are some of your "yes, but..." responses?

_____

_____

_____

_____

_____

_____

_____

2. Go back and review the boxed *Principles* in the previous chapters. Are you willing to allow Jesus to use these principles to bring healing and freedom to *your* life?

_____

_____

Chapter Seventeen

You are my child.
You do not have to be the victim.

White Feathers

He will call upon me, and I will answer him;
I will be with him in trouble, I will deliver
him and honor him. With long life will
I satisfy him and show him my salvation.

PSALM 91:15-16

I was on my face before the Father one morning asking him to show me the areas of darkness in my mind and heart that would keep me from him. There was a lot of confusion in our lives about the direction our ministry was to take. We were waiting for the Lord—always a place of refining. In the midst of my confusion, I was asking him to show me my inadequacies, sins and blind spots. My morning devotion contained the word *cloaked*, so I went before the Father asking him to reveal the hidden things that distressed me. I asked that he help me see them clearly so I could lay them at his feet. You might say my glasses needed cleaning!

As I prayed I began to see a white glowing curtain. It was creamy white with unusual angular lines that intersected to form triangles. The Lord in His glory was on one side of the curtain and I was on the other side. Slowly, dark ooze began to cover the whiteness and I became distressed and fearful. There was a bright red light in the upper right corner that glowed—the tip of a hot poker. As everything went dark, I prayed against the evil. I wanted to go back to the light, but the Lord allowed the darkness to come. It was okay, he said, because I needed to see this. I was back in that dusty, oily garage at my great grandfather's farm. I was on my back in the dirt. One of the drunken men was holding the searing poker near my face so that I would lie still. I was a child, maybe five, and I was being raped. The face I saw was my father's and he was calling me a "bastard child." I experienced that memory for only a few seconds.

The Lord took me quickly behind the white curtain—out of the darkness and into the light. He said, "Ann, you are not a bastard child. You are *my* child. You do not have to be the victim. You are now and forever covered. You do not have to struggle to protect yourself. *I* have always been there to protect and defend you." He then took the hot poker and sealed that garage door shut. It was finished!

Understanding began to dawn. He was trying to teach me to live in the confidence of my safety in him. It is not likely that I will be victimized again the way I was as a child. But on an emotional level there were times when I was behaving as though I was still in danger. I had always defended myself with the "heart of a lion," but that lion sometimes got in people's faces. It was not always meek and gentle. How might I behave differently now that I know the Lord is my protector? I can recognize Satan as the culprit before

I begin defending myself. I can stop and pray and fight for the other person's heart. I can show tenderness; not a *rescuing* tenderness or a *fix-it* mentality, but rather a coming-in-line with the Father's desire for healing and wholeness. I can pray.

In the memory, I was behind that incredibly beautiful white curtain. I was safe. I did not have to defend myself. *God* was in control.

He who dwells in the shelter of the Most High
will rest in the shadow of the Almighty.
I will say of the LORD, "He is my refuge and my fortress,
my God, in whom I trust."
Surely he will save you from the fowler's snare
and from the deadly pestilence.
He will cover you with his feathers,
and under his wings you will find refuge;
his faithfulness will be your shield and rampart.
You will not fear the terror of night,
nor the arrow that flies by day,
nor the pestilence that stalks in the darkness,
nor the plague that destroys at midday.
A thousand may fall at your side,
ten thousand at your right hand,
but it will not come near you.
You will only observe with your eyes
and see the punishment of the wicked.
If you make the Most High your dwelling—
even the LORD, who is my refuge—
then no harm will befall you,
no disaster will come near your tent.
For he will command his angels concerning you

to guard you in all your ways;
they will lift you up in their hands,
so that you will not strike your foot against a stone.
You will tread upon the lion and the cobra;
you will trample the great lion and the serpent.
"Because he loves me," says the LORD, "I will rescue him;
I will protect him, for he acknowledges my name.
He will call upon me, and I will answer him;
I will be with him in trouble,
I will deliver him and honor him.
With long life will I satisfy him
and show him my salvation" (Psalm 91).

As I examined the structure of that white curtain more carefully, I saw that it was not a curtain after all. It was a wing. The angular lines were feathers. Being a retired science teacher, I have a great appreciation for the beautifully complex structure of feathers. The shafts of flight feathers are hollow, making them extremely light. The vanes are barbed so that they latch together to form a durable sheath to lift the bird's weight in flight. On close examination you can see spaces between the barbs (large enough to allow air to circulate) so that a chick under the wing is protected but will not suffocate. The air spaces also provide insulation for warmth. With a little preening, ruffled feathers can be realigned and returned to their appropriate place.

How like the Lord to give me a familiar and intricately detailed picture of his protection of me. In picture and poetry he said, "I am your defender. Trust me!"

Chapter Seventeen

Reflecting on God's Light

1. Reflect on Psalm 91. What comforting words do you find there about God being your protector and defender?

_____

_____

_____

_____

_____

_____

2. Ask the Lord if there are any strongholds of fear that cause you to believe you must protect yourself.

_____

_____

_____

_____

_____

_____

Chapter Eighteen

*I am talking about a laughter that
brings humility and compassion.*

Rediscover Your "Sense of Wonder"

How great is your goodness, which you
have stored up for those who fear you,
which you bestow in the sight of men
on those who take refuge in you.

PSALM 31:19

*L*et me ask you, "What stirs your heart?" Do you love to sing, dance or act? Are you an artist or a sculptor? Maybe you love to sew or ride, decorate or garden? The Lord has created within each of us a need for beauty that we often do not recognize or perhaps ignore because of other demands in life. Passion is an integral part of who we are and we lose a bit of ourselves when that passion is suppressed. Ask the Lord to show you the passions of your heart.

I have a friend who grew up in Detroit. She is a pencil-thin elegant woman who spent her early years in a really rough black neighborhood, but the Lord preserved her life. Lora's passion is to dance, and man, can she dance! She does ballet and ballroom. She does be-bop and rap. She couples her passion for dance with her passion for the Lord.

She captures the attention and then the hearts of young people with a combination of elegance and antics. Then she shares Jesus' love and admonition with them.

This woman has given me a great personal gift. She has taught me to dance a worshipful dance before my God. Having been raised in the Baptist church, teaching me to dance was a real test of her abilities, compassion and fortitude. But I can dance! David danced before the Lord in worship and praise. I can dance, too. Lora used the thing she is passionate about to help set me free to worship the Lord in a totally new and holy way! Passions have a purpose.

Another woman taught me to be spontaneous. Some of my friends will roll their eyes at this, but my nature is to be quiet and reflective. The abuse taught me to be controlled. Spontaneity was not even in my vocabulary. I didn't have a clue how to just do something on the spur of the moment. I was rigid. Mary was an artist and a free spirit. As I allowed a little of her passion to infect my heart, I learned to be more flexible and to enjoy being spontaneous!

If you do not have a passion or a passionate friend, get outside in nature. I always found if I could get my students focused on the minute details of God's creation that their sense of wonder began to grow. It is incredible to watch a snail slide its way across a piece of clear plastic. You will find yourself asking, "How does he do that!?!" If you don't like slimy things, examine a flower with a hand lens. The details are amazing. Go fishing or canoeing. Make snow angels. Become a bird watcher or collect a few bugs. Recently

I discovered that the back of every axis deer (an exotic game deer found in South Texas) has a different pattern of white spots on their wheat-colored coats which allows the babies to identify their mothers. Wow! The beauty of God's work is wonder-filled.

Ask the Lord how he would have you use your passion to touch the lives of others. Another friend of mine uses her skill in quilting to help reach into the lives of women in the rainforests of southern Mexico. She and her husband are missionaries. I do not think she had a passion for quilting at the beginning. But the Lord has used it as an avenue to bring healing to the native women, and she is now passionate about quilting!

Find a Christian woman you can laugh with. Scientific research tells us that laughter produces endorphins, which lift our spirits and heal our bodies. Laughter before the Lord can be a form of worship. It is a statement of, "Here I am Lord with all my baggage, but you call me beautiful and I will praise you." I am talking about a laughter that brings humility and compassion. It is a way of saying to someone else, "He loves and accepts me. Therefore, I can love and accept you, unconditionally. Let me encourage you to live in His freedom!"

Don't neglect to soak yourself in the Word. Write your thoughts, fears, and praises in a journal. It is a means to "remember" the things the Lord does in your life over the years. Remember the oral traditions of the Israelites? The words of this book come, in a large part, from my journals. I look at them and marvel at what the Lord has done, and I am humbled.

The wings of the ostrich flap joyfully,
but they cannot compare with the pinions and feathers
of the stork.
She lays her eggs on the ground
and lets them warm in the sand,
unmindful that a foot may crush them,
that some wild animal may trample them.
She treats her young harshly, as if they were not hers;
she cares not that her labor was in vain,
for God did not endow her with wisdom
or give her a share of good sense.
Yet when she spreads her feathers to run,
she laughs at horse and rider (Job 39:13-18).

This passage always makes me laugh out loud! The ostrich is not lovely or beautiful when compared to the elegant stork. She is not a good housekeeper. Her mothering skills seem unconventional and crude. She is not wise in the ways of the world and has more than a fair share of "blond days." But the Lord designed her with a passion for running, and she can run like the wind! She laughs at the horse and rider as she passes them by!

Can you feel it: the passion, the exhilaration, the destiny, the purpose? What passion has the Lord placed in your heart? Have you engaged that passion, or is it smoldering on the back burner? Go to the Lord and ask him to show you how you may express your passion for living, in him.

Our hearts are designed to receive the things of the Lord. A small step in His direction will help to begin the restoration of your sense of wonder.

Chapter Eighteen

Reflecting on God's Light

1. What are you passionate about? What stirs your heart?

_____

_____

_____

_____

_____

2. What would it take for you to begin using your God-given talents and passion? Devise a plan!

_____

_____

_____

_____

_____

_____

_____

Chapter Nineteen

He has lifted me out of the stinking,
sucking mire and set my feet
on solid ground.

Looking With New Eyes

A new power is in operation. The Spirit of life in Christ, like a strong wind, has magnificently cleared the air, freeing you from a fated lifetime of brutal tyranny at the hands of sin and death.

ROMANS 8:2 THE MESSAGE

As I look at my life these days, I cannot help but *"look with new eyes."* I see myself as the one whose life the Lord preserved, his precious jewel. Satan's lies have been exposed and he has far less ground on which to stand when accusing me. I can distinguish his voice from that of my Father's.

God went for the jugular when he sent his own Son. He didn't deal with the problem as something remote and unimportant. In his Son, Jesus, he personally took on the human condition, entered the disordered mess of struggling humanity in order to set it right once and for all. This resurrection life you received from God is not a timid, grave-tending life. It's adventurously expectant, greeting God with a childlike "What's next, Papa?" God's Spirit touches our spirits and confirms who we really

are. We know who he is, and we know who we are:
Father and children (Romans 8:3,15-16 The Message).

I am confident in my relationship with the Lord. I am passionate about seeking his counsel and receiving his correction as I face each new day. Though the mundane and stressful things are still there, he has become my joy.

We can be so sure that every detail in our lives of love for God is worked into something good (Romans 8:28 The Message).

I can see that the Lord has covered me with his mercy in the midst of the sexual abuse in my life. He was there. He has lifted me out of the stinking, sucking mire and set my feet on solid ground. I am clean and I am free!

As I stand in freedom, I can also *"look with new eyes"* upon my earthly father. He was a painfully wounded man who had an obsessive need for control. I see him only through eyes of sadness for his personal pain, guilt and shame.

My mother shared the guilt of my father's abusive behavior, but she was also a victim of his abuse. I can only see her with eyes of compassion. For a time, she suppressed the memories and refused to release those things to the Lord, unwittingly holding my father and her guilt as idols. They were taking the Lord's place in her life. Now, however, she is moving into wholeness, knowing she is forgiven.

I look around me and I see the walking wounded.

It is not for me to judge but only to show empathy and kindness as the Lord opens doors of opportunity. I feel less and less threatened by the actions of others. There is less anger, less anxiety and I rarely reach for the "orange vest" anymore. As I learn to walk in my new-found freedom, the need to be in control surfaces less often, because I know I can relinquish the lives of the ones I love to the Lord. My husband and children are excited. They have become more secure in the Lord's ability and desire to heal their own wounds because of the evidence of his work in me. Our relationships have become more healthy and whole.

And my Heavenly Father, how do my *"new eyes"* look to Him? I see him as my hiding place, my home. My husband called one evening from Eastern Europe. He had been gone for two weeks. There was a strangled whisper of desperation coming across the thousands of miles of microwaves and metal wires, "I'm ready to come home!" My heart melted. Yes! I know that feeling! That is what I say to the Father when I stub my spiritual toe—"I'm ready to come home." Those are my words when new painful memories begin to surface—"I'm ready to come home." They will be the words in my heart when he finally calls for me—"I am ready to come home."

The words of this song written by my pastor, David Danielson, express the source of my hope and joy—my Heavenly Father.

To See You As You Really Are
David Danielson (October 19-21, 1999)

Childhood pictures projected forward
color the world in which I live;
echoes from the past,
still rippling the waters of my soul, deep within...

but You meet there...
perfect love drives out fear;
I repent, Lord, of judging You.

Shine Your light,
enlighten my eyes
to see You as You really are...
to see You...as You really are.

Expectations created in my youth
still cause my eyes to miss the truth.
The wounded heart of a child within me
still playing hide and seek...

but You meet there...
perfect love drives out fear;
I repent, Lord, of judging You.

Shine Your light,
enlighten my eye
to see You as You really are...
to see You...as You really are.

(USED BY PERMISSION)

I now "call back" to you that

❍   He went with me into the storm.

❍   He kept me.

❍   He bore me up.

❍   My face glows with triumph.

❍   My feet sprint in the race.

❍   He heard my cry.

❍   He saw me through the night.

❍   Come on! He wants to do the same for you!

❍   I am looking with new eyes.

Chapter Nineteen

Reflecting on God's Light

1. What would it take for you to begin *"looking with new eyes?"*

_____

_____

_____

_____

_____

_____

2. Are there things you would need to help you accomplish that goal?

_____

_____

_____

_____

_____

_____

Chapter Twenty

I am "calling back" to you...

Lest I Mislead You...

> *This is what Hezekiah did throughout Judah, doing what was good and right and faithful before the LORD his God. In everything that he undertook in the service of God's temple... he sought his God and worked wholeheartedly. And so he prospered.*

> 2 CHRONICLES 31:20-21

There are several things I feel must be said in closing. Hopefully these thoughts will clarify any misconceptions that may be lingering with the words I have written.

1. Satan is our enemy, but he is already defeated.

The passion of Christ (the thing he desired above all things, regardless of the anguish and pain) was to become the righteous means for you and me to be able to come into the presence of God the Father without falling dead! We bear the rebellious nature of sin within our human bodies and minds. Without Christ's covering and cleansing, our very presence is the stench of death in the nostrils of the Father. Things we do, things done to us and our ungodly choices clothe us in death and bondage. Yet, the passion of Jesus Christ was to take our place—in those rotting grave clothes—so that we could experience the righteous love of God the Father. Christ died in my place and in your place.

The Spirit of God alerts us to our need for reconciliation to the Father in order to be made free and whole. As we approach the throne room of God, Jesus stands at the door saying, "Here, little one, let me wash away the stench of sin and death. I have for you the most fragrant healing oil. It is my blood. The Father cries every time he smells it. Not only is it wonderfully fragrant, but it has the power to clean and mend those rags you are wearing. They will become a robe as white as snow. Then you will be properly dressed to go into the presence of the Father.

When we accept the gift of Christ, we are changed outwardly and inwardly. The healing penetrates all the way to our hearts. All we have to do is allow him to cover us with that wonderfully fragrant oil—his blood.

When we walk into the glory of God's throne room, we are amazed by the beauty and brilliance all around us. Jesus brings us to the Father and says, "This is one you have given me. She is mine. Because she is mine, she is also yours." And God the Father, in all of his awesome and fearful glory, smiles and says, "Come here child. I know you. I have been waiting for you to come. I have such great plans for you..." Thus begins our relationship with the Father, the God of all creation.

Strange as it may seem, crazy and unthinkable as it is, there are days when I will choose to rebel against the Father. Satan smiles that maliciously sly smile and tries to convince himself that he has won a victory. But Satan has no real power over me until I listen to his lies. I give him opportunity by resorting to questioning the Father's character and love, following the example of my sister, Eve.

If we stick close to the Father, he has incredible things to share with us. He will teach us to trust him. He will begin to reveal the depths of his love in ways that make little sense to the human mind. He will redeem our hearts and minds, and ultimately, our bodies. His love will draw us in and fill us up any moment we choose to respond.

Satan is our enemy, but he has always been defeated!

2. Jesus Christ is not only in the business of bringing us into the Father's presence (redeeming us) he also desires to restore us.

In my experience, this process had a pattern.

❍ *I had to recognize that I was a captive to my childhood wounds and that my feelings and behaviors in my adult life were tied to those wounds.*

I had to realize that Jesus had the desire and power to bring healing.

In the book, *Captivating*, John and Stasi Eldredge put it like this:

Let Jesus come in. Open the door and invite him to find us in those hurting places. Healing never comes against our will. In order to experience his healing, we must also give him permission to come to places we have so long shut to anyone. He knocks through our loneliness, our sorrows, and events that feel too close to what happened to us when we were young—betrayal, rejection, abandonment.[1]

I had to recognize that I was captive to those feelings, and be willing to open the door to my hurting heart.

○ *I needed to come to the point where I understood that I believed things about myself that were not true.*

I was not guilty. I was not dirty. I did not need to feel ashamed. I was not abandoned by God. I was not stripped of everything of value and worth. My physical and emotional wounds brought messages, lots of messages. Because they were delivered with such pain, they *felt* true. But they were lies.

○ *I had to allow the Lord to tell me the truth about myself in those painful childhood memories and come into a place of agreement with him.*

It was okay for me to ask, "Where were you, Lord?"

What did Jesus say? "I was there! I suffered *with* you. I suffered *for* you. You are not dirty and shameful. You are lovable. You did not lose everything of value and worth in those awful times. You are *my* child. You are *my* beloved. You are my *Precious Jewel*." With his words came peace, joy and calm.

○ *I had to grieve.*

Grief says the wound mattered, I mattered, and that it was not the way life was supposed to be. It is a form of validation. Each time the Lord brought me to a painful memory, there was grief: grief for the loss of innocence, grief for the fear and pain, grief for the ultimate impact the abuse had on my life.

○ *I had to renounce the vows I made as a child.*

I had made a vow to never be left vulnerable again, a vow to be in control of the things around me so that I (and my family) could be safe. Those vows put *me* on *God's* throne. I was dependent on myself, not trusting God to take care of me. In a very real sense, my ability to control the things around me became my idol. But that idol was not able to keep me safe!

○ *I had to forgive those who hurt me.*

Holding onto bitterness keeps us captive to the wounds. In order for me to be free, the Lord said I had to take off the "prison clothes." I had to turn them loose and walk away. It was my choice. It was a part of the road to freedom. In the book, *Total Forgiveness*, R.T. Kendall writes, "True forgiveness can only be offered after we have come to terms with reality."[2] I had done that. It was no longer my job to hold my offenders accountable. That job belongs to God. He says, *Love...keeps no record of wrongs* (1 Corinthians 13:5).

○ *Each new day I must choose to walk in the freedom the Lord has given me.*

I am in the process of learning his ways and leaving behind old habits. It requires desire and discipline in order for change to take place. The desire springs from my close relationship with my Father—to please him, to experience the joy of being his child, to be open to the moving of his Spirit. The discipline follows, naturally, out of that relationship. I have a new way of life, one that includes joy and peace in the midst of a broken world.

3. Deep inner healing takes time and commitment.

Healing is not dependent upon anyone other than you and Jesus Christ. During the three-year period covered in this book, I was ministered to by at least seven different people: some were licensed counselors, some were prayer ministers, at times it was me and the Lord alone. If there are serious abuse issues in your past, I do not recommend that you approach deep inner healing alone. Seek the partnership of others. In the appendix I have listed a number of places you might choose to start.

Are you brave enough to begin the journey to healing and freedom? If you are, then ponder, again, these promises the Lord gave me through the words of Frances Roberts:

> The limitations of your natural vision will be no handicap. The Spirit is not detained by the flesh. The Spirit will move in spite of the flesh and will accomplish a renewal and do a work of re-creating, so that the newly liberated creature will rise up in virgin life,

starting out upon a ministry the foundation of which no man has laid. It will be a path of holiness, a way of miracles, and a life of glory. You will see My shining smile.

Nothing will be required of you but obedience. You will follow the call of the Spirit and not search for the path; for the way will be laid down before you as you tread. Wherever you stop, there will the path stop also. Whenever you walk in faith, the way will be made clear before you.

Be as a young child and step out in confidence, knowing that with your hand in Mine you will be always safe, and blessings will attend you.[3]

Be encouraged. I have walked this path of obedience and the Lord has shown himself to be faithful, trustworthy, loving and kind—every step along the way. I have *sought God and worked wholeheartedly... and* I have *prospered*. I am walking in *his* freedom and I am *Looking With New Eyes*.

I am "calling back" to you, "You can have his freedom, too!"

Chapter Twenty

Reflecting on God's Light

Dallas Willard says transformation starts with a vision, must be pursued with intention and requires a means for completion.[4]

1. What is your vision for transforming your life?

_____

_____

_____

_____

_____

_____

2. How do you intend to pursue that vision?

_____

_____

_____

_____

_____

_____

3. What means are necessary for the vision to become reality?

_____

_____

_____

_____

_____

_____

Endnotes

Introduction

[1] Cowman, L.B. *Streams in the Desert.* Grand Rapids, MI: Zondervan Publishing House, 1997, 470.

[2] Willard, Dallas. *Renovation of the Heart: A Video Resource for Groups.* Franklin Springs, GA: Life Springs Resources, 2003.

Chapter 1

[1] Roberts, Frances J. *Come Away My Beloved.* Uhrichsville, OH: Barbour Books, 2002, 211-212.

Chapter 2

[1] Jakes, T.D. *Woman, Thou Art Loosed!* New York, NY: International Press, 1997, 40.

[2] Smith, Edward M. *Healing Life's Hurts Through Theophostic Prayer.* Ventura, CA: Regal Books, 2002, 27.

Chapter 3

[1] Smith, 30.

[2] Kraft, Charles H. *Defeating Dark Angels: Breaking Through Oppression In the Believer's Life.* Ann Arbor, MI: Servant Publications, 1992.

Chapter 4

[1] Smith, 28.

Chapter 5

[1] Pink, Arthur W. *Satan and His Gospel.* Swengel, PA: Reiner Publications, 26.

[2] *The Passion of the Christ.* NewMarket Films. Icon Productions, 2004.

[3] *Broken Trust: For Survivors of Sexual Abuse* (American Association of Christian Counselors Video). Chicago, IL: Christian Counseling Resources, Inc., 1996.

[4] Smith, 66.

[5] Jakes, 31-33.

[6] Allender, Dan B. and Temper Longman III. *The Cry of the Soul: How Our Emotions Reveal Our Deepest Questions About God.* Colorado Springs, CO: Navpress, 1990, 44.

Chapter 6

[1] Nouwen, Henri J.M. *The Return of the Prodigal Son.* New York, NY: Doubleday, 1992, 50.

[2] Smith, 29.

[3] Nouwen, 54.

Chapter 7

[1] Frangipane, Francis. *The Three Battlegrounds.* Cedar Rapids, IA: Arrow Publications, 1989, 47.

[2] Roberts, 105.

Chapter 9

[1] Smith, 30.

[2] Smith, 30.

[3] Strong, James. *The New Strong's Exhaustive*

Concordance of the Bible. Nashville, TN: Thomas Nelson Publishers, 1984, 28.

Chapter 10

[1] Smith, 31-32.

Chapter 11

[1] Willard.

[2] Chambers, Oswald. *The Utmost for His Highest (Classic Edition).* Uhrichsville, OH: Barbour Books.

Chapter 12

[1] Smith, 30.

[2] Smith, 32.

[3] Smith, 33.

Chapter 13

[1] Smith, 32.

Chapter 14

[1] Smith, 33.

Chapter 15

[1] Nouwen, 51.

[2] Nouwen, 53.

[3] Nouwen, 53.

[4] Nouwen, 54.

[5] Nouwen, 55.

[6] Nouwen, 55.

Chapter 16

[1] Eldredge, John. *Waking the Dead.* Nashville, TN: Nelson Books, 2003, 87.

Chapter 20

[1] Eldredge, John and Stasi Eldredge. *Captivating: Unveiling the Mystery of a Woman's Soul.* Nashville, TN: Nelson Books, 2005, 100.

[2] Kendall, R.T. *Total Forgiveness.* Lake Mary, FL: Charisma House, 2002, 16.

[3] Roberts, 211-212.

[4] Willard.

Bibliography

Allender, Dan B. *The Wounded Heart: Hope for Adult Victims of Childhood Sexual Abuse.* Colorado Springs, CO: Navpress, 1990.

Allender, Dan B. and Temper Longman III. *The Cry of the Soul: How Our Emotions Reveal Our Deepest Questions About God.* Colorado Springs, CO: Navpress, 1990.

Anderson, Neil A. *Released From Bondage.* Nashville, TN: Thomas Nelson Publishers, 1993.

Broken Trust: For Survivors of Sexual Abuse (American Association of Christian Counselors Video). Chicago, IL: Christian Counseling Resources, Inc., 1996.

Chambers, Oswald. *My Utmost for His Highest (Classic Edition).* Uhrichsville, OH: Barbour Books.

Coates, Jan. *Set Free: God's Healing Power for Abuse Survivors and Those Who Love Them.* Minneapolis, MN: Bethany House Publishers, 2005.

Cowman, L.B. *Streams in the Desert.* Grand Rapids, MI: Zondervan Publishing House, 1997.

Kraft, Charles H. *Defeating Dark Angels: Breaking Through Oppression In the Believer's Life.* Ann Arbor, MI: Servant Publications, 1992.

Eldredge, John. *Waking the Dead.* Nashville, TN: Nelson

Books, 2003.

Eldredge, John and Stasi Eldredge. *Captivating: Unveiling the Mystery of a Woman's Soul.* Nashville, TN: Nelson Books, 2005.

Frangipane, Francis. *The Three Battlegrounds.* Cedar Rapids, IA: Arrow Publications, 1989.

Freyd, Jennifer J. *Betrayal Trauma.* Cambridge, MA: Harvard University Press, 1996.

Haddock, Deborah Bray. *The Dissociative Identity Disorder Sourcebook.* Chicago, IL: Contemporary Books, 2001.

Jakes, T.D. *Woman Thou Art Loosed!* New York, NY: International Press, 1997.

Kendall, R.T. *Total Forgiveness.* Lake Mary, FL: Charisma House, 2002.

Nouwen, Henri J.M. *The Return of the Prodigal Son.* New York, NY: Doubleday, 1992.

Pink, Arthur W. *Satan and His Gospel.* Swengel, PA: Reiner Publications.

Roberts, Frances J. *Come Away My Beloved.* Uhrichsville, OH: Barbour Books, 2002.

Sands, Christa. *Learning to Trust Again.* Grand Rapids, MI: Discovery House Publishers, 1999.

Smith, Edward M. *Healing Life's Hurts Through Theophostic Prayer.* Ventura, CA: Regal Books, 2002.

Strong, James. *The New Strong's Exhaustive Concordance of the Bible.* Nashville, TN: Thomas Nelson Publishers, 1984.

Tuggle, Brad and Cheryl. *A Healing Marriage: Biblical Help for Overcoming Childhood Sexual Abuse.* Colorado Springs, CO: Navpress, 2004.

Willard, Dallas. *Renovation of the Heart: A Video Resource for Groups.* Franklin Springs, GA: Life Springs Resources, 2003.

Resources

For additional information on or possible assistance with the type of prayer ministry described in this book, you may contact one of the following resources:

Mount Horeb House
P.O. Box 293722
Kerrville, TX 78029
www.mounthorebministries.com
ageroy@ktc.com

Faith Family Ministries
Restoration Retreat
P.O. Box 1200
Blue Ridge, GA 30513
www.faithfamily.net
ffm@faithfamily.net

Theophostic Ministries
P.O. Box 489
Campbellsville, KY 42719
www.theophostic.com
phostic@kyol.net

Note: Annette Geroy is not officially affiliated with Theophostic Ministries.